Resurrection of the Flesh
or Resurrection from the Dead

Resurrection of the Flesh
or Resurrection from the Dead

Implications for Theology

Brian Schmisek

A Michael Glazier Book

LITURGICAL PRESS

Collegeville, Minnesota

www.litpress.org

A Michael Glazier Book published by Liturgical Press

Cover design by Jodi Hendrickson. Mosaic by Marnie Simmons.

The illustration, "The World of the Hebrews," is reprinted by permission of Catholic Book Publishing Corp.

Excerpts from documents of the Second Vatican Council are from *Vatican Council II: The Basic Sixteen Documents*, by Austin Flannery, OP, © 1996 (Costello Publishing Company, Inc.). Used with permission.

Excerpts from the Greek New Testament and author's translation thereof are from *Novum Testamentum graece*, 27th ed., edited by E. Nestle and K. Aland, © 1993 (Deutsche Bibelstiftung).

Translations of church fathers and other theologians are author's own, unless otherwise noted.

Unless otherwise noted, Scripture texts in this work are taken from the *New Revised Standard Version Bible* © 1989, Division of Christian Education of the National Council of the Churches of Christ in the United States of America. Used by permission. All rights reserved.

1   2   3   4   5   6   7   8   9

Library of Congress Cataloging-in-Publication Data

Schmisek, Brian.
    Resurrection of the flesh, or, resurrection from the dead :
implications for theology / Brian Schmisek.
      pages   cm
      "A Michael Glazier book."
      Includes bibliographical references and index.
      ISBN 978-0-8146-8224-1 (pbk. : alk. paper) — ISBN 978-0-8146-8249-4 (e-book)
    1. Resurrection.   2. Catholic Church—Doctrines.   I. Title.
    BT873.S36   2013
    236'.8—dc23   2013007687

To my wife Marnie and our four precious children—
John, Clare, Peter, and Helen:

*Your lives are a greater witness to the glory of God
and the wonders of the universe than any text.*

Contents

Preface

This book arose from my interest in grasping a better under-standing of Paul's enigmatic term in 1 Corinthians 15:44: "spiritual body." My research into the matter, which was also the topic of my dissertation, coincided with opportunities to speak to audiences of lay Catholics about resurrection. I spoke at various parishes, pre-sented workshops at religious education gatherings (including the 2011 Religious Education Congress in Anaheim), delivered papers at several academic conferences, and taught brief courses on the topic. By making a conscious decision to write a short book that is likely to be read by a wide audience, I hope this work combines the fruits of scholarship with an easy tone — that is, not laden with impenetrable theological jargon.

Fine academic colleagues and friends at the University of Dal-las, Jerome Walsh, John Norris, Mark Goodwin, Pat Madden, and Andrew Glicksman, were kind in reading numerous drafts of chapters 1 and 2. Their remarks and wise counsel were valuable. A fall 2009 adult education class on the topic of resurrection at the University of Dallas School of Ministry was filled with inquiring and inquisitive people of faith. Their questions, comments, and insights influenced this work in various ways. Thanks are also in order for a dear friend, Jonathan Lunine at Cornell University, who read the pages concerning our scientific understanding of the universe. His eye saved me from some embarrassing errors. Another friend and colleague at the University of Dallas, Robert Kugelmann, read the section on the human person and offered new ways of considering the material. Peter Gilmour, whom I am proud to now call a colleague at Loyola University Chicago, read the manu-script in its entirety and offered helpful suggestions. The profession-alism and diligence of the editorial team at Liturgical Press, Nicole Werner, Lauren L. Murphy, Colleen Stiller, and Hans Christoffersen, made the process both efficient and a delight. With so many friends, colleagues, students, mentors, and others to review the material it goes without saying that any oversights or errors that remain are due solely to my own shortcomings. This book is a product of the efforts outlined above and more.

I also wish to acknowledge and thank Deacon Denis Simon who encouraged me for many years to make a Holy Week retreat with the Jesuits at Montserrat near Lake Dallas. Due primarily to his prompting and generosity, I made two retreats there in three years. Those fruitful days provided some uninterrupted time to think about the topic of resurrection and the book itself without the many distractions of daily life.

This book is written for the believer who struggles with the concept of resurrection in light of modern scientific knowledge. It is assumed that the reader possesses a basic knowledge of Scripture, theology, and some church teaching but is not an expert. It is also assumed that the reader is a believing Catholic, though the book may also appeal to other Christians. The book was not written to convince a nonbeliever of the resurrection of Jesus. Instead, I hope this book opens up for a believer the possibility of understanding resurrection in different ways, though still consistent with the apostolic witness and church teaching. I humbly recognize "the instrinsic provisionality" of this endeavor and offer this work to the church as a whole "for scrutiny and evaluation" (TTPPC, 47).

Abbreviations

AB   Anchor Bible

AugSt   *Augustinian Studies*

BDAG   W. Bauer, F. W. Danker, W. F. Arndt, and F. W. Gingrich. *Greek-English Lexicon of the New Testament and Other Early Christian Literature.* 3rd ed. Revised and edited by F. W. Danker. Chicago: University of Chicago Press, 2000.

BDB   F. Brown, S. R. Driver, and C. A. Briggs. *A Hebrew and English Lexicon of the Old Testament.* Oxford: Clarendon, 1952.

BDF   F. Blass, A. Debrunner, and R. W. Funk. *A Greek Grammar of the New Testament and Other Early Christian Literature.* Translated by R. W. Funk. Chicago: University of Chicago Press, 1961.

BTB   *Biblical Theology Bulletin*

CBQ   *Catholic Biblical Quarterly*

CCSL   Corpus Christianorum: series latina

CSEL   *Corpus scriptorum ecclesiasticorum latinorum*

DS   H. Denzinger and A. Schönmetzer. *Enchiridion symbolorum definitionum et declarationum de rebus fidei et morum.* 35th ed. Rome: Herder, 1973.

DTC   A Vacant and E. Mangenot. *Dictionnaire de théologie catholique.* Paris: Letouzey and Ané, 1908.

DV   *Dei Verbum,* Vatican Council II (November 18, 1965).

GS   *Gaudium et Spes,* Vatican Council II (December 7, 1965).

HNTE   *Handbuch zum Neuen Testament,* Ergänzungsband

JBL   *Journal of Biblical Literature*

JTS   *Journal of Theological Studies*

KJV   King James Version

LCQCE   *Letter on Certain Questions Concerning Eschatology.* Congre-
          gation for the Doctrine of the Faith (May 17, 1979), http://www
          .doctrinafidei.va/documents/rc_con_cfaith_doc_19790517
          _escatologia_en.html.

LG   *Lumen Gentium*, Vatican Council II (November 21, 1964).

MFC   Message of the Fathers of the Church

N-A²⁷   E. Nestle and K. Aland, eds., *Novum Testamentum graece*,
          27th ed. (Stuttgart: Deutsche Bibelstiftung, 1993).

NABRE   New American Bible, Revised Edition

NJBC   R. E. Brown, J. A. Fitzmyer, and R. E. Murphy. *The New
          Jerome Biblical Commentary.* Englewood Cliffs, NJ: Prentice
          Hall, 1990.

OED   *Oxford English Dictionary.* 3rd edition, December 2001;
          www.oed.com.

PMS   Patristic Monograph Series

PNAS   Proceedings of the National Academy of the Sciences

SBLMS   Society of Biblical Literature Monograph Series

SEAug   Studia ephemeridis Augustinianum

TTPPC   Theology Today: Perspectives, Principles, and Criteria.
          International Theological Commission. (November 29, 2011),
          http://www.vatican.va/roman_curia/congregations
          /cfaith/cti_documents/rc_cti_doc_20111129_teologia-oggi
          _en.html.

UCPCP   University of California Publications in Classical Philology

USCCA   *United States Catholic Catechism for Adults* (Washington, DC:
          United States Conference of Catholic Bishops, 2006).

VC   *Vigiliae christianae*

Abbreviations of Primary Sources

1 Clem.	*1 Clement*
2 Clem.	*2 Clement*
Aeschylus, *Ag.*	Aeschylus, *Agamemnon*

Aeschylus, *Eum.*	Aeschylus, *Eumenides*
Aristotle, *De An.*	Aristotle, *De Anima*
Aristotle, *Pol.*	Aristotle, *Politics*
Eusebius, *Hist. eccl.*	Eusebius, *Historia Ecclesiastica*
Homer, *Il.*	Homer, *Iliad*
Ignatius, *Eph.*	Ignatius, *To the Ephesians*
Ignatius, *Mag.*	Ignatius, *To the Magnesians*
Ignatius, *Pol.*	Ignatius, *To Polycarp*
Ignatius, *Smyrn.*	Ignatius, *To the Smyrnaeans*
Ignatius, *Trall.*	Ignatius, *To the Trallians*
Irenaeus, *AH*	Irenaeus, *Adversus Haereses*
Justin Martyr, *1 Apol.*	Justin Martyr, *1 Apology*
Justin Martyr, *2 Apol.*	Justin Martyr, *2 Apology*
Justin Martyr, *Dial.*	Justin Martyr, *Dialogue with Trypho*
LXX	Septuagint
Plato, *Cra.*	Plato, *Cratylus*
Plato, *Grg.*	Plato, *Gorgias*
Plato, *Phd.*	Plato, *Phaedo*
Plato, *Phaedr.*	Plato, *Phaedrus*
Plato, *Phileb.*	Plato, *Philebus*
Polycarp, *Phil.*	Polycarp, *To the Philippians*
Ps. Sol.	*Psalms of Solomon*
Sophocles, *El.*	Sophocles, *Electra*
T. Levi	*Testament of Levi*

Chapter 1

A History of Interpreting Resurrection

Introduction

"We believe in the true resurrection of this flesh that we now possess." These words from the thirteenth-century Council of Lyons are quoted in the second edition of the Catechism of the Catholic Church (1017). Yet, do Christians really believe in the resurrection of the flesh that we now possess? What age will I be when I am raised? Will I be raised with a thirty-year-old body, a fifty-year-old body, a seventy-year-old body? What if my corpse is cremated? How does the flesh return? Will I have all my parts? Will I need digestive organs? To what end? Will I need eyes to see? Will I need hair? What hair would return when I have had so many haircuts throughout my life? Will I have a beard if I had one in this life? Such questions arise naturally. These questions vex not only us but also our forebears in faith. Thinking about the afterlife often causes confusion and wonder.

A pudgy preaching pastor proclaimed to his parishioners that in the heavenly realm we will all have adult, fit bodies, not needing food or drink and being perfectly happy without these earthly necessities. He concluded by quipping, "At least I hope so. I don't want to be dragging this three-hundred-pound body around for all eternity!" The congregation laughed, and one person approached the pastor after Mass. She told him that she agreed with his assessment since "we will all be angels after we die." The pastor told her that was not what "we" believe. An interesting discussion ensued as it had in earlier generations and as it will in later generations. Christians today are influenced in their attitudes about the afterlife by cinematic portrayals such as *Ghost* and *What Dreams May Come* as much as they are by the New Testament or even Sunday preaching.

But ultimately we ask: Does a belief in the raising of this very flesh conform to a biblical understanding of resurrection? Is such a belief reflected by the apostolic witness? How might the biblical text inform the language used to speak of resurrection in a pastoral context today? How might the witness of the New Testament cause us to rethink our preconceptions about resurrection?

The three chapters of this book deal with (1) a brief historical survey of the Christian understanding of resurrection, (2) an examination of the biblical data (especially New Testament) regarding resurrection, and (3) a brief review of some modern ways we look at the world. The book concludes with some thoughts about how we might understand resurrection today.

History

[handwritten: Jesus Resurrection → met w/ misunderstanding one flesh lang. introd'd → repeated over & over]

The resurrection of Jesus is a central tenet of Christianity. "If Christ has not been raised, your faith is futile," says the Apostle Paul (1 Cor 15:17). Yet, from New Testament times, resurrection has been met with misunderstanding (2 Tim 2:18), opposition (Acts 17:32), and downright rejection (1 Cor 15:12). Theologians beginning with Paul in the latter half of 1 Corinthians, chapter 15, have attempted to define the resurrection in more detail. At times, antagonists who denied the resurrection caused this desire for a definition. At other times, theologians addressed the topic in commentaries on Scripture without any reference to an ongoing denial. Often theologians simply repeated verbatim what earlier theologians said. Significantly, from a very early period in church history, theologians began to speak of the resurrection of the flesh instead of the resurrection from the dead. Once "flesh" language was used to speak of resurrection, it was repeated, and repeated, and repeated to the present day. In doing so, a graphic, physical understanding of the resurrection was implanted in the Christian imagination.

Apostolic Fathers

The early church writers and thinkers who followed the apostles are often referred to as the Apostolic Fathers. Though the term comes from the seventeenth century, it has been a useful way of referring to this group of writers and writings. There is some debate about who is actually on the list, but in general, the following are the core group: First Clement, Second Clement, Didache (The Teaching of

[handwritten: Apostolic Fathers – gen'lly writing to fellow-Christians]

the Twelve Apostles), Polycarp, Ignatius of Antioch, Epistle of Barnabas, The Martyrdom of Polycarp, Epistle to Diognetus, and Papias (fragments). The Apostolic Fathers wrote primarily to an internal audience. That is to say, they were writing to fellow Christians, for whom resurrection was not a divisive issue. In fact, resurrection is mentioned only a few times in the entire corpus of the Apostolic Fathers. Perhaps Polycarp sums up the attitude best when he says that whoever would deny the resurrection is the firstborn of Satan (7.1). Stated simply, there was not much philosophical reflection on the "how" of the resurrection. Instead, the Apostolic Fathers were content to preach the "that" of resurrection.

[handwritten: – not much mention of Resurrect'n – accept'd as fact – didn't consider 'how' much]

1 Clement

The *First Letter of Clement* (referred to as *1 Clem.*) is so-named by the early church, even though the letter contains no direct reference to Clement's authorship. The Clement for whom it is named was a bishop of Rome from 92 to 101 CE, according to Eusebius's chronology.[1] The date of composition often given for *1 Clem.* is 95 or 96 CE, though there is a broader consensus for somewhere between 80 and 140 CE.

Like other Apostolic Fathers, resurrection was not a major issue for Clement and he spent little time discussing it. He saw that the way the natural world worked (for example the daily rising of the sun) indicated that there would be a coming resurrection (*1 Clem.* 24.1). This early predilection for using the natural world to bear witness to resurrection was also seen in Paul (1 Cor 15). So Clement was in good company by doing so. However, Clement also did something new. He apparently felt at liberty to use new imagery different from that of the New Testament to speak of resurrection. In perhaps the most imaginative presentation of resurrection among the Apostolic Fathers, Clement was the first Christian to relate resurrection to the image of the Phoenix rising from its own ashes (*1 Clem.* 25).

There are many different versions of the story of the Phoenix. In Clement's telling of the story, the Phoenix lives five hundred years before preparing its own place of death, a coffin-like nest. Once it dies and the flesh begins to decay, a worm is born that feeds on the

[handwritten: Clement → described Resurrection to Phoenix rising from ashes]

[1] Eusebius, *Hist. eccl.*, 3.15.34.

—Used nature & pagan imagery

corpse, eventually growing wings. The creature carries the nest with the bones of the Phoenix and flies to Heliopolis in Egypt where the priests of the temple of the sun are able to inspect it. This story, which may sound rather strange, demonstrates for Clement the power of God. Resurrection should not sound so fantastic when compared to the life, death, and rebirth of the Phoenix.

And yet, Clement did not spell out the nature of his resurrection anthropology in any extant writings. Thus it seems that the earliest generation of post–New Testament authors felt free to draw on pagan imagery to convey the concept of resurrection. Rather than simply reciting formulas or teachings that had been handed on to him, Clement was comfortable using examples from nature and even from pagan tradition, which perhaps was common imagery for his audience.

Ignatius of Antioch

Ignatius of Antioch wrote seven letters to Christian churches on his way to martyrdom at Rome. Eusebius dated his martyrdom during the Roman Emperor Trajan's reign (98–117 CE), about 107 CE, though many modern scholars have placed the date somewhere in the latter part of Trajan's reign (110–17 CE).

Ignatius may have been one of the first to stress the fleshly characteristics of the resurrected Christ (*Smyrn.* 3.1-3; 12.2). In fact, Ignatius speaks of "flesh and spirit" often when speaking of Christ.[2] For Ignatius, flesh represents the sphere of corruptibility rather than that of sin. Thus, he saw in Christ a spiritual transformation of all that is fleshly.[3] So, passages such as *Smyr.* 3.3, "And after his resurrection he ate and drank with them like someone composed of flesh, although spiritually he was united with the Father," seem to echo Luke's image of the risen Christ and also foreshadowed the later christological debates of the fourth and fifth centuries.[4] This stress on the fleshly aspect of the resurrection gave rise to more physical

---

[2] J. E. McWilliam-Dewart cites Ignatius, *Eph.* 7.2, *Mag.* 13.3, *Trall.* Salutation, *Smyrn.* 12.2, and *Pol.* 1.2 and 2.2 in *Death and Resurrection*, MFC 22 (Wilmington, DE: M. Glazier, 1986), 49.

[3] W. R. Schoedel, *Ignatius of Antioch: A Commentary on the Letters of Ignatius of Antioch*, Hermeneia (Philadelphia: Fortress Press, 1985), 23.

[4] Ibid., 20.

understandings of Christ's resurrection, and thus to the resurrection of believers.

Didache

Didache or *"The Teaching of the (Lord through the Twelve) Apostles (to the Nations)"* is a work of ethical (chaps. 1–6) and liturgical (chaps. 7–15) instruction concluded by an eschatological teaching (chap. 16). It has been called "the most important document of the subapostolic period."[5] The only reference to resurrection in *Didache* is 16.6. In this verse, the author of *Didache* reviews the signs of truth that will appear before the Lord comes upon the clouds of heaven. The sign is a rift in heaven, followed by the signal of a trumpet call. The third is the resurrection of the dead. The author immediately adds, "not of all, however, but as it has been said, 'The Lord will come and all the holy ones with him'" (16.7). Some scholars believe that this resurrection could refer to the thousand-year reign of Christ mentioned in Revelation 20:4-6.[6] Indeed, later church fathers such as Justin Martyr and Irenaeus maintained a physical resurrection hand-in-hand with their millennial expectations.

The author of *Didache* generally did not delve into speculative matters.[7] It is no surprise, then, that one finds no speculation in *Didache* on the nature of the resurrection, much less on the nature of the resurrected body. Significantly, the author of *Didache* preserved the language of the New Testament, which often uses the phrase "resurrection of the dead."

Polycarp

Though Polycarp (d. ca. 155–60 CE) was one of the more significant figures of early Christianity, he had little to say about resurrection in his one extant letter. In short, the resurrection was for Polycarp a fundamental aspect of the faith. "For anyone who does not confess that Jesus Christ has come in the flesh is an antichrist. And whoever does not confess the testimony of the cross is from the devil. And whoever

---

[5] J. Quasten, *Patrology*, vol. 1 (Westminster, MD: Newman, 1950–60), 30.

[6] E.g., R. Knopf, *Die Lehre der zwölf Apostel. Die zwei Clemensbriefe*, HNTE, *Die Apostolischen Väter* 1 (Tübingen: Mohr-Siebeck, 1920), 40.

[7] K. Niederwimmer, *The Didache*, Hermeneia (Minneapolis, MN: Fortress, 1998), 228.

perverts the sayings of the Lord for his own desires and says that there is no resurrection or judgment is the firstborn of Satan" (*Phil.* 7.1).

2 Clement

The so-called *Second Letter of Clement* was probably not written by Clement and is not so much a letter as it is a sermon or homily given in Corinth around 98 to 100 CE.[8]

A significant development in the way theologians expressed the resurrection took place in *2 Clem.* The author insists that if Christ won salvation in the flesh and thus called them (the audience), they "in this flesh" would receive their reward (9.5). Thus, a shift from Paul's term "spiritual body" (1 Cor 15:44) occurred in the language used by *2 Clem.* to speak of the resurrection. Moreover, this shift may have occurred within the Corinthian community itself in less than fifty years from the time Paul wrote of the resurrection in terms of spiritual body. It would then seem that the problems Paul dealt with in Corinth concerning the resurrection still persisted in the following generations of the Christian Corinthian community. But regardless of its date of composition, *2 Clem.* addresses a problem where some members denied that the flesh was judged or that it rose. In an effort to address this problem, the author of *2 Clem.* uses language not found in Paul or even elsewhere in the New Testament to discuss resurrection. That term is *flesh*.

Apologists

While the Apostolic Fathers wrote primarily to those within the believing community, the apologists in the latter half of the second

---

[8] The general hypothesis for the composition and dating of this document has been advanced by K. Donfried who believed that the Roman church's intervention (*1 Clem.*) into the Corinthian congregation's problems was successful. The previously deposed Corinthian elders were reinstated. *2 Clement* is a hortatory address delivered by one such previously deposed elder on the occasion of the resolution of the crisis. See K. P. Donfried, *The Setting of Second Clement in Early Christianity* (Leiden: E.J. Brill, 1974), 1–48. It should be noted, however, that not all scholars share this view. E.g., Quasten believed that *2 Clement*'s opinion of penance gives reason to date the work as "not long after the *Shepherd of Hermas*, that is, about 150 AD" (Quasten, *Patrology*, 1. 54).

century wrote mostly to those outside the church. The apologists defended Christianity against persecutions and pagan accusations. Apologetic literature flourished in the second and third centuries and continued even after the political victory of Christianity in the Roman Empire.

The apologists, especially Justin Martyr and Irenaeus, cast Christian faith in the Greek philosophical categories of the day in part so that the educated classes of Greek and Roman society would see the logic or reasonableness of Christian faith. By doing this, the apologists set Christian faith on a trajectory that nearly inextricably linked the faith to a Greek philosophical system, as we shall see.

Perhaps the two greatest philosophers of ancient Greece were Plato and Aristotle. Their influence on Western Civilization, especially philosophy and Christian theology, can hardly be overstated. Indeed, they may have had as much influence on Christian theology in the West as the Bible itself. For our purposes, their anthropological ideas are of particular interest. They (and many others) had fierce debates as to the nature of the soul.

In simplistic terms, Plato saw a sharp division between body and soul (e.g., *Phd.* 91d), with the soul existing prior to the body[9] and living eternally after the body's death. In fact, Plato seems to borrow language from earlier authors when he claims that the body (*sōma*) is the tomb, or shell (*sēma*) for the soul.[10] "In fact I once heard sages say that we are now dead, and the body [*sōma*] is a tomb [*sēma*] for us, and the part of the soul [*psychēs*] in which there are desires is of the sort to be swayed and to vacillate to and fro."[11] So, though Plato viewed the body (*sōma*) as a unified whole (*Phaedr.* 264c; cf. *Phileb.* 29a–b), the body is not the whole of a person.

For Aristotle, the term "soul" could refer to the principle of life in all living things. A living thing is an "ensouled body" or a "body with a soul," *empsychon sōma.* For Aristotle, the living being is body and

---

[9] "The [soul] that has shed its wings is carried along until it fastens onto something solid, where once settled, takes upon itself an earthly body [*sōma*], which seems because of the power of the soul [*psychē*] to move itself; it is called a living being, and the whole, soul and body joined together, has the name mortal." Plato, *Phaedr.* 246c.

[10] Plato, *Phaedr.* 250c; *Cra.* 400b–c.

[11] Plato, *Grg.* 493a.

soul, inseparable—e.g., "so the soul and body together constitute a living being. Therefore, the soul cannot be separated from the body."[12]

Aristotle believed that plants, animals, and humans had souls suited to them. In other words, Aristotle believed that there were plant souls, animal souls, and human souls. Plants have the lowest level of soul, concerned primarily with reproduction and nutrition. Animals have a higher ordered soul, possessing desire, sense, and motion, in addition to reproduction and nutrition. Human beings have the highest of all souls, possessing, in addition, reason, which governs the lower ordered qualities (reproduction, desire, etc). The mind, rather than the soul, is eternal.[13]

For Aristotle, the body and soul are related to one another intimately as form and matter; the soul is the form of the body.[14] The body is temporally prior to the soul with respect to its development.[15] While Aristotle moved beyond what Plato had proposed, neither of them had any idea of the biblical or ancient Israelite view that understood animals and human beings to have the "breath of life" and, therefore, enjoy the status of "living" (cf. Gen 2:7; 6:17; 7:4; Job 12:10). Plants are not living beings according to ancient Israelite thought. "Body and soul" is not a term used with any regularity in the New Testament

[12] Aristotle, *De An.*, 2.1. 413a.

[13] Ibid., 3.5. 430a.

[14] "Indeed, we call one certain kind of thing substance. There is the sense as matter, that which by itself is not 'this.' There is another sense, shape and form, that by which something is already called 'this.' There is a third sense, which is each of the two senses together. . . . So, every physical body that has life could be a substance, substance in the sense of a composite. But since it is a body of such and such a kind, for it has life, the body cannot be soul; for the body is not those things attributed to it, but rather the subject or matter. So the soul must be a substance in the sense of the form of a natural body having life potentiality within it." Aristotle, *De An.*, 2.1. 412a.

[15] "And as the body [*sōma*] is prior to the soul [*psychēs*] with respect to its development, so also the irrational is prior to the rational. And this is the proof: for temper, will, and even desire, are present in children as soon as they come into the world, but reason and intellect develop in them as they grow older. Therefore in the first place it is necessary for the training of the body [*sōmatos*] to precede that of the soul [*psychēs*], and then the training of desire; but the training of the desire must be for the sake of the intellect, and that of the body [*sōmatos*] for the sake of the soul [*psychēs*]." Aristotle, *Pol.*, 7.15, 1334b, 20–21.

to express the human being. In fact, in the entire New Testament, the terms "body" and "soul" are used together in only five verses.[16]

Thus, the apologists attempted to recast biblical or Christian faith in Greek terms and imagery. By doing so, they set the trajectory for later Christian theology. Augustine, for example, was heavily influenced by platonic thought. Thomas Aquinas was more influenced by Aristotle. In modern times, scholars have had recourse to the Bible itself to incorporate its anthropological ideas into theology.

Justin Martyr

Justin (100–165 CE) was born at Flavia Neapolis (present-day Nablus) in Palestine and eventually suffered a martyr's death. He was educated in stoic, Pythagorean, platonic, and peripatetic philosophical schools (*Dial* 2.1–6). He later became a Christian and went to Rome, where he wrote his only extant works, *Dialogue with Trypho* and *1 and 2 Apology*. In them, he taught a resurrection of the flesh. His life, thought, and works influenced his own and subsequent generations. For example, Tatian the Assyrian was numbered among his disciples.

Justin seems to have been the first to apply the adjective "second" (*deutera*) to "coming" (*parousia*) (*1 Apol.* 52.3). Thus, the idea of Christ's second coming heavily influenced Justin's eschatology. He believed in a resurrection of the saints followed by their one thousand–year reign in Jerusalem, known as "millennialism." At the end of that thousand-year reign, the wicked would be raised, and all would experience a final judgment (*Dial* 80.5; 81.4). Thus, Justin believed the resurrection of the dead was a corollary of millennialism, placing him in two eschatological traditions. First, he believed that human bodies would be revived and assume immortality (*1 Apol.* 18–19). Second, he believed in the immortality of the soul (*Dial.* 105). These two eschatological traditions were woven into his millennialism,

---

[16] The passages are Matthew 6:25 (par Luke 12:22-23), 1 Thessalonians 5:23, Revelation 18:13, and Matthew 10:28, which alone is the closest thing we find in the New Testament to a Greek duality between body and soul: "Do not fear those who kill the body [*sōma*] but cannot kill the soul [*psychēn*]; rather fear him who can destroy both soul [*psychēn*] and body [*sōma*] in hell" (Matt 10:28). The fact that one verse in the entire New Testament reflects this anthropology demonstrates how meager its influence was.

which, in turn, facilitated his understanding of a physical, bodily resurrection. In his *Dialogue*, Justin used the phrases "resurrection of the dead" (45.1; 80.4; 82.1) and "resurrection of the flesh" (80.5), thereby wedding Christianity to Greek philosophical categories. By doing so he solved certain problems but created others that later generations would address.

Tatian

Tatian (ca. 120–180 CE) was an Assyrian convert to Christianity. He knew and was influenced by Justin Martyr until Justin's death, at which time Tatian seems to have become a Gnostic.[17] He was then regarded as a heretic, which is why nearly none of his work survives. The only surviving work in its original language is the *Address to the Greeks*. In it, Tatian taught that the flesh would rise again with its eternal soul: "Therefore, the soul of human beings consists of many parts, and it is not a single thing. For it is a composite, so that it is visible because of the body. For it would never appear by itself without the body; nor does the flesh rise without the soul" (15).

Irenaeus

Irenaeus (130–202 CE) was a pupil of Polycarp, the Apostolic Father mentioned above. Irenaeus, like Justin Martyr, was also a millennialist, though his concepts were different from those of Justin in that Irenaeus believed in a six thousand–year reign.

> For in as many days as this world came into being, in so many thousand years shall it be concluded. . . . This is both an account of the things formerly created, how they came to be, as it is also a prophecy of what is to come. For if the day of the Lord is as a thousand years, and in six days the created things were completed, it is clear that their conclusion is the sixth thousandth year. (Irenaeus, *AH* 5.28.3; see also 5.29.2)

---

[17] The Greek term "Gnostic" means "learned" or "one who knows," and it applies to some early Christians who held beliefs that were later deemed heretical, such as salvation of the soul from the material world through learning or knowledge.

In the fifth book of his major work, *Against Heresies*, Irenaeus had the most to say about resurrection. His Gnostic opponents seem to have used 1 Corinthians 15:44 to argue for a spiritual resurrection as opposed to a fleshly resurrection (Irenaeus, *AH* 5.7.1–2). Even though Irenaeus speaks of spiritual bodies as those animal bodies that have been vivified by the Spirit to perpetual life, his concept of the resurrected body was truly that of *flesh*: "They will indeed rise in the flesh, although unwillingly, in order to acknowledge the power of the one who stirs them up from the dead" (Irenaeus, *AH* 1.22.1). His argumentation moved beyond the power of God to the Incarnation itself. Since the Word of God was flesh, our own flesh will see salvation. "If flesh did not have to be saved, the Word of God would never have been made flesh. And if the blood of the just had not been sought after, the Lord would never have had blood" (Irenaeus, *AH* 5.14.1). Furthermore, Irenaeus argued that the flesh has the hope of resurrection, having received the Eucharist.

> However, how can they say again that the flesh, which is nourished by the body and blood of the Lord, goes to corruption and does not partake of life? Therefore, let them either change their opinion or abstain from offering what has just been said. However, our opinion is in harmony with the Eucharist, and the Eucharist in turn confirms our opinion. Indeed, we offer to him what is his, harmoniously declaring the participation and union of the flesh and Spirit. For just as the bread that is from the earth, when it receives the invocation of God, is no longer common bread, but the Eucharist, consisting of two realities, earthly and heavenly, so also our bodies, receiving the Eucharist, are no longer corruptible, but have the hope of resurrection. (Irenaeus, *AH* 4.18.5; see also 5.2.3)

The millennial tendencies of Irenaeus seem to have shaped his physical view of the resurrected body, leaving no doubt that Irenaeus believed in a resurrection of this earthly, fleshly body.

Athenagoras

It was Athenagoras (ca. 133–90 CE), a professional philosopher who lived in Athens and a contemporary of Tatian, who wrote the first Christian treatise specifically on this subject, aptly titled *On the Resurrection*. Since he makes no mention of Christ and does cite the pagan physician Galen, he probably addressed the work to non-Christians. In it he discusses crass, physical problems associated with resurrection. For example, if a human being consumes an animal that itself had consumed a human being, how will God keep the parts straight at the resurrection (*Res.* 4)?[18] His answer was that this task would not be difficult for God, the creator of the world (*Res.* 2–3; 9). In fact, Athenagoras believed that since human beings are body and soul, eternal human existence demands not merely an immortal soul but also a resurrected body (*Res.* 15.2). Moreover, the resurrected bodies would be made of reconstituted parts from their own earthly bodies, "for the bodies that rise up do so with their own reconstituted parts" (*Res.* 7). This led later theologians to wonder whether God might use one's former arm to make that same one's resurrected leg or whether a former arm would have to be resurrected as an arm. In the end, although Athenagoras did not use the term "resurrection of the flesh," he did envision a restoration of the material body.

> It is absolutely necessary that there be a resurrection of the bodies which have died or have even been entirely dissolved, and the same human beings must emerge again. . . . But the same human beings cannot emerge again unless the same bodies are restored to the same souls. (*Res.* 25.3)

Tertullian

Tertullian (b. ca. 160 CE) was born a pagan in Carthage. He became a Christian by 197 and was ordained a priest around 200. Sometime after 206 Tertullian seems to have become a Montanist.[19] By 213 he had completely separated from the church and later from the Montanists, forming his own sect. Augustine later reconciled the Tertullianists with the church. Tertullian's writings on the resurrection, most of which he wrote after 206, drew heavily from Irenaeus. Like his contemporaries, Tertullian claimed a resurrection of the flesh (e.g., *On Resurrection*, 56.1). In fact, he saw the resurrection as that of the flesh to such a degree that he claimed Lazarus as "the pre-eminent

---

[18] Known as the chain-consumption argument.

[19] A Montanist is a member of an early-Christian movement named after its founder, Montanus. Montanism was later declared heretical.

instance of resurrection."[20] Tertullian did not query Lazarus's dying after this resurrection. Tertullian also cited certain statements of faith from the period that used the phrase "resurrection of the flesh."[21]

One sees the development that has taken place up to this point. Paul spoke of the resurrection in terms of "spiritual body." The Apostolic Fathers stressed that Christ was in the flesh. Since he was in the flesh and rose in the flesh, Christians too will rise in the flesh.

Tertullian began to read Paul as one who taught the resurrection of the flesh, even though the term appears nowhere in the Pauline corpus. "But when he calls Christ 'the last Adam,' recognize from this that he works to establish with all the force of his teaching the resurrection of the flesh, not of the soul."[22] It appears that an understanding of a fleshly resurrection arose because Gnostics and, perhaps, other non-Christians were denying the resurrection by asking probing questions, such as the "chain-consumption" argument. The apologists responded that anything is possible for God. To those who denied resurrection in the flesh on other grounds (e.g., flesh is not worthy of resurrection), the apologists stressed the unity of the human person, divine justice, and the consequent necessity of the resurrection of the flesh. Despite this strong, growing tradition of a fleshly resurrection, the claim was not accepted by all as Origen demonstrated.

Origen and His Opponents

Origen was the greatest Christian thinker of his day and perhaps the greatest Christian thinker at that time since Paul. Origen (185–253 CE) was born in Alexandria, a major center of intellectual activity in early Christianity. His father, who educated Origen in Christianity and Greek literature, was martyred in a persecution ordered by Emperor Septimius Severus in 202. Origen led a long and distinguished career in writing and commenting on the Scriptures. He traveled extensively, teaching and preaching in many different places including Rome, Athens, Caesarea Maritima, and Arabia. In 250, the emperor Decius began a persecution of Christians, although he seemed to want apostates rather than martyrs. While many Christians did defect,

---

[20] Tertullian, *De Resurrectione*, 53.3

[21] E.g., Tertullian, *De praescriptione*, 36; *De virginibus velandis*, 1.3.

[22] Tertullian, *De Resurrectione*, 53.12.

Origen was imprisoned and tortured at Caesarea but did not recant his faith. The emperor Decius died in 251 along with the persecution. Origen died in 253, not long after his release.

Origen contributed a great deal to the discussion on the nature of the resurrected body. His thinking formed something of a wedge between early and late thinkers. Jerome, for example, initially seemed to accept many of Origen's points only to reject them later as nearly heretical. It is difficult to know with certainty what Origen's ideas concerning the nature of the resurrected body were because (a) his treatise on the resurrection has been lost, (b) pertinent passages in other works survive only in Latin translations, and (c) he has been often misquoted and/or misinterpreted by later theologians.[23]

Origen

Origen seems to have been the first Christian theologian to introduce into the discussion of the resurrection the fact that the body is constantly changing, though it retains its form (*eidos*). Humans change throughout their lives: human hair and nails grow, food is consumed and waste is passed. Thus, Origen claimed that "river"[24] was an appropriate name for the body. In doing this he held two opposing concepts together: identity and change. He built on the idea of consistent form *and* change by saying that our spiritual bodies will have the same form (*eidos*) as our bodies do now, though the change they will experience will be for the better. Features that once existed in the flesh will remain in the spiritual body. Origen did not believe that the resurrected body would be simply an incorruptible body of flesh — "it will be flesh no more"[25] — but rather a soul needed a body suited to its environment. For example, Origen claimed we would need gills were we to live underwater, so those who inherit the kingdom of heaven and live in superior places must have spiritual bodies.[26]

---

[23] J. F. Dechow, *Dogma and Mysticism and in Early Christianity: Epiphanius of Cyprus and the Legacy of Origen*, PMS 13 (Macon, GA: Mercer University, 1988), 112.

[24] Origen, *Commentary on Psalms*, Psalm 1.

[25] Ibid.

[26] Ibid.

Thus, Origen's positing of the form (*eidos*) answered the objections of the chain-consumption argument. He rejected "resurrection of the flesh" language while reaffirming the Pauline language of "spiritual body." His ideas were also attractive to later Eastern theologians, while those in the West attacked his arguments as a denial of the resurrection. Many monastic communities in Palestine and Egypt accepted Origen's beliefs throughout the third and fourth centuries. In his commentary on Matthew, Origen says that the resurrected bodies of the blessed would become "like the bodies of angels, ethereal and of shining light."[27] Ideas such as this may have been the basis for his condemnation by later theologians. Origen and followers of Origenism were often accused of a belief in the preexistence of souls. For one holding such a belief, a future resurrection of the body might seem to be something of an oddity.

Another passage of Origen that may have fueled opposition is found in his treatise *On Prayer* (31.3), wherein he denies that the resurrected body would have corporeal knees but affirms that the heavenly body would be spherical. Origen said that anyone who would deny this does not understand the implication of that denial, as he or she would need to claim that intestines and the rectum would function even in heaven.

Though Origen answered the major objections to resurrection in his day, the question of the physicality of the resurrection remained. One of Origen's staunchest and most vocal critics was Methodius.

Methodius

Little is known of Methodius's life (d. ca. 311 CE). His writings are probably from the late third and early fourth centuries. He seems to have been martyred during the persecution of the emperor Diocletian.[28] Methodius's work on the resurrection survives and is significant because he attempts to show the fallacies of Origenism, but modern scholars have often criticized it for misrepresenting many

---

[27] Origen, *Commentary on Matthew*.

[28] J. W. Trigg, *Origen* (The Early Church Fathers; London and New York: Routledge, 1998), 65.

of Origen's positions.[29] It is striking that Methodius denied intrinsic organic change. He believed that food ingested into the human body simply passed through the human body; it did not become bone, sinews, or other bodily organs. He believed that the nutriment replaced only bodily fluids, such as sweat, menstrual fluid, or blood (*On Resurrection*, 2.11–13). A modern person is most likely to see in Methodius the challenges produced by a lack of knowledge in basic natural sciences. Perhaps today we take for granted a post–scientific revolution outlook on the world. We must remind ourselves that the ancients did not have our scientific worldview or, if we don't, we will end up looking upon Methodius, for example, as a foolish thinker. Indeed, Methodius even denied that a tree receives nourishment from the ground. His *via negativa* argument stated that if trees did receive nourishment from the ground, there would be holes around the roots.

> For really how does the entire earth, having entered through the roots into the trunks of trees, and having been divided up through the pores into all the branches, change into leaves and fruit? . . . If it were true that the earth is made into trees as it is brought up through the roots, every place around them would necessarily be emptied of earth. (*On Resurrection*, 2.9)

In Methodius's opinion, organic change for the good is caused by God rather than food. Methodius, like Tertullian before him, believed that flesh would be raised precisely because of the incarnation.

> But if anyone would dare to say that the earthly image is the flesh itself, but the heavenly image some other spiritual body besides the flesh, let him first recall that Christ, the heavenly man, appeared bearing the same form [of body and] of limbs, image, and the same flesh as ours. Because of it, though he was not man, he became man in order that just as in Adam all die, so also in Christ all will be brought to life [1 Cor 15:22]. For if he bore flesh not in order to set it free and raise it up, why did he even bear flesh at all, if he intended neither to save it nor to raise it up? (*On Resurrection*, 2.18)

---

[29] E.g., C. W. Bynum. *The Resurrection of the Body in Western Christianity, 200–1336* (Cambridge University Press, 1995), 68–71.

Methodius rejected Origen's spiritualizing the resurrection in favor of a physical, fleshly resurrection. Anti-Origenist attacks continued in the church, culminating in the Second Council of Constantinople (553), where Origen was condemned as a heretic in the eleventh canon,[30] though some regard his name as a later insertion.[31]

Methodius's work was cited in the fourth century by Epiphanius, bishop of Cyprus (ca. 315–402). He called Origen a heretic, and associated him with Arianism, another movement in the early church that was later declared heretical. Epiphanius was gravely concerned about orthodoxy. He went out of his way to ensure that teachings he considered orthodox were being upheld. At times he meddled in the affairs of nearby bishops, even opposing (in 394) the ordination of Bishop John of Jerusalem because he suspected him of Origenism. Epiphanius published the *Panarion*, a "medicine chest," to use against the sickness of heresy. In book 64 of his *Panarion* he addresses the ills of Origenism. The power that Epiphanius wielded at the time can hardly be underestimated. In the case of Jerome and Rufinus, two powerful theologians who were once friends, Epiphanius was able to draw them into a lifelong bitter dispute. Epiphanius went to Constantinople in 402 to oppose John Chrysostom because he was also suspected of Origenism. Though more of a theological policeman than a theologian, Epiphanius was a bishop who seems to have used his power in an unorthodox fashion. Ultimately, it was the thinking of Jerome and Augustine, who used ideas of earlier theologians in claiming a resurrection of the flesh (even to the point of coining the term "spiritual flesh" as we will see below), who would form the basis of medieval scholastic thinking.

---

[30] "If anyone does not anathemitize Arius, Eunomius, Macedonius, Apollinaris, Nestorius, Eutyches, and Origen, with their ungodly writings, and all the other heretics who are condemned by the holy catholic and apostolic church and by the previously mentioned four holy synods, and [does not anathemitize] those who have held or now hold similar opinions to these previously mentioned heretics and in their impiety persist to the end: let him be anathema." DS 433.

[31] *DTC* 3, p. 1251–52.

Church Fathers

"Church fathers" is the name given to a group of theologians who lived and wrote in the fourth and fifth centuries. The study of the church fathers is called patristics. Sometimes patristics is understood broadly to include Apostolic Fathers to the early middle ages. The term is used more strictly here. We will highlight three church fathers: Jerome, Gregory of Nyssa, and Augustine. Perhaps contrary to popular opinion, the church fathers were not in complete unanimity on many issues of their day. They fought fiercely, called each other names, held grudges, and occasionally reconciled. Though many of their differences are papered over today, it is good to recall that they discussed and debated their ideas about God, Jesus, Scripture, and the church.

Jerome

Jerome (340–420 CE) was born in a town near the border of Pannonia and Dalmatia near modern day Slovenia. He was baptized in Rome around 360. He eventually settled in Bethlehem in 386, where he led a life of austerity and study. He was a prolific writer and translated the Scriptures into Latin. His writings concerning the Origenist matter are preserved in his *Apology against Rufinus* and his *Letters against Rufinus*.

Jerome had been a defender and translator of Origen. Jerome and his friend Rufinus became entangled in a dispute between Bishop John of Jerusalem and Bishop Epiphanius of Cyprus. Epiphanius accused John of Origenism. When monks sent by Epiphanius requested Jerome to disavow Origenism, he complied, but Rufinus refused to see these same monks,[32] thus beginning their conflict. The debate between the two was so bitter and acrimonious that they died at odds, despite various attempts and a brief success at reconciliation.

Jerome indicated clearly that he expected a resurrection of this earthly body. He even revealed some of the arguments that were used by his opponents.

> And to those of us who ask whether the resurrection will exhibit from its former condition hair and teeth, the chest and the

[32] J. N. D. Kelly, *Jerome: His Life, Writings, and Controversies* (Peabody, MA: Hendrickson, 1998), 198.

stomach, hands and feet, and other joints, then, no longer able to contain themselves and their jollity, they burst out laughing and adding insult to injury they ask if we shall need barbers, and cakes, and doctors, and cobblers, and whether we believe that the genitalia of which sex would rise, whether our (men's) cheeks would rise rough, while women's would be soft and whether the bodies would be differentiated based on sex. Because, if we surrender this point, they immediately proceed to female genitalia and everything else in and around the womb. They deny that singular members of the body rise, but the body, which is constituted from members, they say rises. (*Letters* 84.5)

It is clear that Jerome expected the resurrection of this earthly, fleshly body.

Gregory of Nyssa

Gregory (d. ca. 386 CE) was born into a devout Christian family: his maternal grandmother was a martyr, two of his brothers became bishops, and his sister Macrina is honored as a saint. Gregory seems to have married, and later (371) to have been made the bishop of Nyssa. His thinking was bold, and he broke much new ground, though his influence on the debate concerning the resurrected body was not great, as later theologians, and even he himself, did not advance many of his ideas concerning the resurrection.[33]

Gregory of Nyssa defended the resurrection of the body, while at times using Origenist language to do so. He borrowed Origen's idea of *eidos* (the one distinct form of the body that is preserved at the resurrection) but claimed that the *eidos*, being allied to the soul in this life, remained imprinted on it in the next. Thus, the elements that make up the body are recognized by the soul at death, since they bear the seal of the *eidos*. In this way, the body is raised, being composed in the resurrection of the same elements it bore in this life.

Now to that part of the soul that is in the likeness of God, it is not a stream of some sort that is changed, but it is this steadfast

[33] E.g., Gregory theorizes in his *Oratio de mortuis* that a person's virtue or vice in this life determines the form of the resurrected body. Later theologians did not discuss this theory to a great degree, much less advance it. Again, in his early works he posited new understandings of Origen's *eidos* concept, never to refer to them again.

and stable element in our composition fastened to it. And since diverse variations of composition are transformed into differences according to form (the composition is simply the mixture of the elements, and we say elements are the foundation for the apparatus of everything, even the human body), while the form by necessity endures in the soul as in the impression of a seal, the soul recognizes those things that have been stamped with the seal, but at the time of the re-formation the soul receives again the very things which correspond to the stamp of the form: and all those things which were stamped in the beginning by the form would so correspond. So, it is not unreasonable that what belongs to the individual should again return to it from the common source.[34]

Gregory transformed Origen's idea of *eidos* into his own — i.e., that which provides the means for the reassembly of the body's elements at the resurrection. Origen, of course, would have denied Gregory's postulation that *eidos* is that which allows precisely the same elements constituting the earthly body to make up the resurrected body.

In Gregory's work specifically on the resurrection, *De Anima*, he argued that no matter how finely dissolved the parts of the dead human body were, the soul would keep up with each part, awaiting the signal from God to restore these parts to the whole.

[The soul] remains after dissolution in those elements in which it existed from the beginning, and, like a guardian placed over private property, it does not abandon them when they are mingled with kindred elements. But, by the keen ubiquity of its intellectual power it abides patiently in the dissolution of the straying elements. It joins the kindred elements with its own mixed up elements. It is not exhausted by keeping up with them when they are poured back into the universe. Rather, it remains in them always, wherever and however nature arranges them. And if there should be a signal from the power that arranges everything that the dissolute elements combine again, then as various ropes fastened together at one starting point, they likewise all respond to the pull at the same time. So in like manner, by the one power of the soul, when there is a pulling of the various elements, sud-

---

[34] Gregory of Nyssa, *De Hominis Opificio*, 27.

denly, in the coming together of the private property, the cord of our body will be twisted together with the soul, each returning to its former neighbor and embracing what is familiar.[35]

Any separated elements are united to reform the dissolved being by producing the same person.

Such is the difference [between us and those outside our philosophy]: we assert that the same body, put together from the same elements, is constructed again around the soul . . . he disagrees in thinking that the bodies are not made out of the same elements as those which grew around the soul via the flesh in the beginning.[36]

Gregory believed that this resurrected body would not be afflicted with any weaknesses experienced by the human body. In fact, the resurrected body would be a body similar to Adam and Eve's before the Fall. In this work and in many others he claimed, "the resurrection is nothing other than the restoration of our nature to its original condition."[37]

In *De mortuis*, an early work, Gregory displays himself as a bold theologian and advances a new idea on the nature of the resurrected body. The form of the resurrected body will be determined by the virtues or vices of the individual, much as the facial expression in one's earthly life is a reflection of one's inner disposition. Thus, one's inner moral state will become one's outer form, showing the sort of person one is. In other words, the good rise beautiful whereas the bad rise ugly!

Just as at present the variation of the elements in us determine the differences of each one's characteristics, with each changing his shape or the color of his complexion based on more or less of the arranged elements, so it seems to me, the factors determining the form of each person then will not be these elements. Rather, his own qualities of evil or virtue will become explicit, and their unique combination one way or the other will create the form.[38]

---

[35] Gregory of Nyssa, *De Anima*.

[36] Ibid.

[37] Ibid.; see also Gregory of Nyssa, *De Hominis Opificio*, 17.

[38] Gregory of Nyssa, *De Anima*.

It is important to remember that Gregory argued with Methodius against Origen in *De Anima* and *De Hominis Opificio*, while in *De Mortuis*, written at an earlier point in his career, he is strongly influenced by Origen.[39] In *De Mortuis*, Gregory seems to have such a disparaging view of the body, that some have queried why he defended the resurrection at all.[40] Others such as Jean Daniélou explains Gregory's position in relation to Origen as this: "For Origen, the physical body and the spiritual body are two different bodies. For Gregory, the two are states of the same body."[41]

In summary, Gregory expressed different concepts of the resurrection in different works. He seemed content not to advance in later works many of the ideas he expressed earlier. He did advance the notion of the resurrected body in physical terms, although at times

---

[39] T. J. Dennis, "Gregory on the Resurrection of the Body" in *The Easter Sermons of Gregory of Nyssa: Translation and Commentary*, eds. A. Spira and C. Klock (Cambridge, MA: Philadelphia Patristic Foundation, Ltd., 1981), 68.

[40] For example, H. Cherniss said: "It is obvious that in the majority of cases Gregory speaks like a Platonist who believed in the necessary cleansing of the soul; but now and again he recalls the fact that his Church requires him to support the dogma of the resurrection and punishment of the body. In that situation Gregory uses an argument hinted at by Plotinus: We are clearly a combination of soul and body; the soul without the body would not sin; therefore, the body must be punished as the seducer of the soul, as well as for its sin in its own right. That this in incompatible with the doctrine of punishment as cure is not to be wondered at; after building up a philosophy of some consistency Gregory is again and again forced to relinquish it or abjure the dogma of corporeal resurrection. . . . So much would be clearly and consistently Gregory's doctrine were it not for the accepted Christian dogma of the resurrection of the body. One feels that Gregory was not happy when he came to this distressing problem which for him meant no less than the absurdity of hoisting the corporeal nature up into the intelligible world." H. F. Cherniss, *The Platonism of Gregory of Nyssa*, UCPCP 11 (1930; repr., New York: Burt Franklin, 1971), 56–57. McWilliam-Dewart also wonders why Gregory defended a fleshly resurrection (*Death and Resurrection*, 156); Dennis maintains that for Gregory the resurrection of the body was a necessity because the body is an essential part of man's nature and that it can contribute to the life to be enjoyed in the hereafter ("Gregory on the Resurrection of the Body," 69).

[41] J. Daniélou, "La resurrection des corps chez Grégoire de Nysse," *VC* 7 (1953): 170.

he seems to place such emphasis on the identification of one's true self with the soul that many scholars have questioned the need in his theology for resurrection. Gregory borrowed Origen's use of *eidos* but completely transformed its meaning, thus revealing his own view of the resurrected body in the afterlife. Furthermore, Gregory compared the resurrected body to that of Adam and Eve before the Fall. Thus, he spoke of resurrection as "the restoration of our original nature." It is not surprising, then, that few theologians followed his line of thinking. In fact, Augustine responded and challenged the idea of resurrection as a restoration of our original nature, though it is unclear whether he had Gregory in mind while doing so.

Augustine

Augustine (354–430 CE), like a majority of his theological predecessors, accepted a physical understanding of the resurrected body's nature. He disagreed, however, with those who would argue for a body like that of Adam and Eve prior to the Fall. Augustine believed that Adam had a natural body rather than a spiritual body.[42]

> For the animal body is prior, of the sort that the first Adam had, though it would not have been subject to death had he not sinned. It is the sort that we ourselves have now, so far has its nature been changed and vitiated, to the extent that he was in that [body], after he sinned, he was changed, so that now the body has the necessity of dying.[43]

Augustine claimed that had Adam obeyed God, he would have inherited a spiritual body as a reward for that obedience: "however, the first man was from the earth, earthly. He was made into a living being, not into a life-giving spirit, for that was saved for him as a reward for obedience."[44] Thus, at the resurrection human beings will not have the body of the first man before sin, because the first man

---

[42] In an earlier article I detailed Augustine's use of this enigmatic Pauline term. Cf. B. Schmisek, "Augustine's Use of 'Spiritual Body'" *AugSt* 35:2 (2004): 237–52.

[43] Augustine, *City of God* 13.23.

[44] Ibid. Later in this same passage Augustine reiterated this point by saying that had he not sinned, Adam would have had an animal body "until it became spiritual, as a reward for obedience" (13.23).

did not have a spiritual body. Augustine cited 1 Corinthians 15:45 to prove that Adam was a living being, while Christ, possessing a spiritual body, was now a life-giving spirit. The spiritual body is a priori, not the body Adam possessed before the Fall.

> We are not at all to think that in the resurrection we shall have such a body as the first man had before sin; nor is that which is said, "As the earthly one, so also those who are earthly," to be understood as that which resulted by the commission of sin. For it must not be considered that prior to his sin he had a spiritual body, and that because of the sin it was changed into an animal body. For if this is thought to be the case, then the words of so great a doctor have been given scant attention, who says, "If there is an animal body there is also a spiritual, as it is written, The first man Adam was made a living being."[45]

Augustine discouraged positive speculation on the nature of the resurrected body.

> Therefore, brothers, let no one inquire with a perverse kind of subtlety what the form of bodies will be in the resurrection of the dead, what stature, what movement, what gait it will have. It is sufficient for you to know that your flesh rises in that form in which the Lord appeared, that is, in human form.[46]

Though he was adamant in his warning, Augustine himself posited certain characteristics of the resurrected body. For example, he believed that spiritual bodies would be supported in existence by a life-giving spirit, which in turn would preserve the body from corruption or lethargy, "so those bodies are called spiritual, but that does not mean that we believe they will be spirits; rather bodies having the substance of flesh. Yet [they] will not suffer any sluggishness or corruption of the flesh since a spirit vivifies them."[47] This idea, or variations of it, has had many twentieth-century proponents.

Augustine stated plainly: "we say that the flesh rises again,"[48] even though he saw some difficulty in 1 Corinthians 15:50: "for flesh and

---

[45] Ibid.
[46] Augustine, Sermon 362.25.27.
[47] Augustine, *City of God*, 13.23.
[48] Augustine, Sermon, 362.13.

blood cannot inherit the kingdom of God." Thus he claimed that at the resurrection we shall possess flesh, rather than be possessed by it.

> Therefore, when we will have risen, flesh will not carry us, but we will carry it. If we carry ourselves we will possess it. If we will possess it, we will not be possessed by it. Because freed from the devil we are the kingdom of God, and so flesh and blood will not possess the kingdom of God.[49]

Later in this sermon, Augustine clarified his position by saying that the resurrected flesh will not be corruptible; indeed, the very name corruption will not apply to flesh and blood.

> The proper name of flesh and blood will also cease to exist; because they are names that apply to mortality. . . . However, the body, because it is not now mortal, is not properly called flesh and blood, because bodies are earthly; rather, it is called a body that is now said to be celestial. . . . Because the flesh in rising again will be changed into such a body that there will no longer be mortal corruption, and for that reason there will be no name of flesh and of blood.[50]

Thus, although Augustine discouraged speculation on the characteristics of the resurrected body, he did discuss the topic at length. Moreover, he addressed questions that had vexed earlier theologians such as the chain-consumption argument and what happened to hair and nails at the resurrection. Augustine claimed that hair or nails that have been lost will be a part of the resurrected body, though not necessarily as hair or nails, for that would be grotesque. Rather, God uses the material as he sees fit in our resurrected body.

> Therefore this earthly material, which becomes a corpse when the soul leaves it, will not at the resurrection be so restored that as a result those things which deteriorated and were turned into various things of different kinds and forms, although they do return to the body from which they deteriorated, must necessarily return to the same parts of the body where they originally were. Otherwise, if what is returned to the hair is that which repeated clippings removed, and if what is returned to the nails is that

[49] Ibid., 362.14.
[50] Ibid., 362.18.21.

which frequent cuttings have pared away, then to those who think, the image becomes gross and indecent, and for that reason it seems to those who do not believe in the resurrection of the flesh to be hideous. But just as if a statue of some soluble metal were melted by fire, pulverized into dust, or mixed together into a mass, and a craftsman wanted to restore it from the same quantity of matter, it would make no difference with respect to its integrity what particle of matter is returned to which part of the statue, provided that the restored statue resumed the whole of the original. So God, the craftsman, shall restore wondrously and ineffably the flesh and with wonderful and ineffable swiftness from the whole of which it originally consisted. Nor will it be of any concern for its restoration whether hairs return to hairs, and nails to nails, or whether whatever of these that had perished be changed into flesh, and be assigned to other parts of the body, for the providence of the craftsman will take care lest anything be indecent.[51]

The gross physical character of this discussion is astonishing for one who discouraged positive speculation on the resurrected body. The modern reader immediately recognizes that Augustine does not share our notions of biology. We understand the human body differently today. This simple fact will have a profound impact on our later discussion. Chapter 91 as well as chapter 89 are influential in later resurrection debates, so it is beneficial to reproduce a portion of chapter 91 here:

Therefore, the bodies of the saints will rise again without any defect, without any deformity, without any corruption, burden, and difficulty, in which ease of movement shall be as complete as their happiness. Because of this, the bodies have been called spiritual, since without a doubt they shall be bodies and not spirits. For just as now the body is called animal, though it is a body, and not a soul, so then the body will be called spiritual, though it will be a body, not a spirit. . . . But regarding the substance, even then it will be flesh. For even after the resurrection the body of Christ was called flesh. The apostle, therefore, says: "It is sown an animal body; it is raised a spiritual body;" because then such will be the harmony between flesh and spirit, as the spirit sustains the subjugated flesh without the need of any nourishment, that no part of our nature will be in discord

---

[51] Augustine, *Enchiridion*, 89.

with another; but just as we shall be free from outside enemies, so we will not have ourselves as enemies within.[52]

Besides the *Enchiridion*, the twenty-second book of the *City of God* was also influential in later resurrection debates. In these books, he discussed whether aborted fetuses would be raised, whether infants would be raised as infants or adults, whether women would retain their sex at the resurrection, or whether the obese would be raised in their obesity. The questions reflected the underlying presuppositions regarding a fleshly, physical resurrection. In this same chapter of *City of God*, Augustine claimed that the spiritual body would be spiritual flesh. "Therefore the spiritual flesh [*caro spiritalis*] will be subjected to the spirit, but it will still be flesh, not spirit. . . . But, man will be spiritual even in body, since the same flesh will have arisen again, so it will be as it is written: 'it is sown a natural body, it will be raised a spiritual body.'"[53]

Thus, by the time Augustine died, the basic framework for discussing the resurrection in later centuries was established. Though Augustine used the term "spiritual body," he meant by it a resurrection involving flesh. Augustine's influence on later theologians who discussed the resurrection can hardly be understated.

Scholastics

The section on scholastics includes a small but representative group of authors who contributed to the discussion on the nature of the resurrected body. Most of their work followed patristic writers — Augustine in particular. A prominent feature of the scholastic debate was their understanding of body and soul and how that understanding affected their language to speak of resurrection.

Peter Lombard

Peter (ca. 1100–1160 CE) was born in Italy and studied in Bologna, Rheims, and Paris. It is believed that Peter wrote his *Sentences* sometime between 1146 and 1151. Though he wrote many other works, the

---

[52] Ibid.

[53] Augustine, *City of God*, 22.21 (CCSL 48.481). Cf. *Contra Duas Epistulas Pelagionorum* 1,10.17 (CSEL 60.439).

Sentences formed something of a textbook for later scholastic theology. As a result, this theological work gave him a place in the history of medieval studies. He accepted the bishopric of Paris in 1158 or 1159 CE, but resigned it shortly thereafter, and died shortly after that.

In the section on the resurrection, distinctions 43–50 in the fourth book of his *Sentences*, Peter borrowed heavily from Augustine's *Enchiridion*: chapter 2 of distinction 44 is basically Augustine's *Enchiridion* 88–89, chapter 3 of distinction 44 is the first part of Augustine's *Enchiridion* 91, and chapter 4 corresponds to *Enchiridion* 92, while chapter 5 reflects Augustine's *City of God* 22.5. Although some modern commentators have regarded Peter's discussion on the resurrection as something of an afterthought,[54] his discussion is significant for two reasons. Since he discussed the resurrection near the end of his work, later theologians who followed the structure of his *Sentences* (e.g. Aquinas) placed the discussion of resurrection at the end of their works. Second, though he was certainly not the first to do so, he quoted Augustine heavily, a practice that later theologians also adopted.

Hugh of St. Victor

Hugh (ca. 1096–1141 CE) was born and died in Saxony. At a young age he joined the Canons Regular of St. Augustine. His uncle, the Bishop of Halberstadt, directed him to go to the monastery of St. Victor in Paris. He arrived in 1115, became head of the school in 1133, and remained there until his death in 1141.

Of the many works of Hugh of St. Victor, there remains a treatise *De Sacramentis*, wherein he comments on the resurrection.[55] Hugh was so familiar with St. Augustine's writings that he was known as *alter Augustinus* (the other Augustine).[56] Indeed, one chapter seems to have been taken from Augustine's *Enchiridion* 91,[57] and other chapters

---

[54] E.g., C. W. Bynum, *The Resurrection of the Body*, 124.

[55] Part 17 of book 2 in Hugh's work is titled "On the End of the Age." In this part, he discussed such topics as whether aborted children shall rise, what will be the nature of Siamese twins, at what age infants shall rise, whether the *reprobi*, "wicked," shall rise with their vices and deformities, and how the earthly will abide in heaven.

[56] R. J. Deferrari, *Hugh of Saint Victor on the Sacraments of the Christian Faith (De Sacramentis)*. (Cambridge, MA: The Mediaeval Academy of America, 1951), ix.

[57] Hugh of Saint Victor, *De Sacramentis*, 2.17.17.

seem to have been dependent on Augustine's *City of God* 22.[58] Besides having borrowed heavily from Augustine, Hugh maintained that the substance of the spiritual body would be flesh.

> But if I will rise in an airy body, then it will not be I who rise. For how is it a true resurrection if the flesh is not able to be true? There fore, clear reasoning suggests that, if the flesh will not be true, then certainly the resurrection will not be true. For a proper resurrection cannot be said to exist where what has fallen does not rise.[59]

He entertained the arguments of those who discussed whether all the particles that have made up one's earthly body would be restored to the resurrected body. Hugh believed that they could be so restored, though each hair particle would not have to return as another hair particle; God is able to effect the resurrection as he sees fit.[60] Despite the fact that Hugh believed the resurrected body to be of flesh, he also posited that it would dwell in the heavens (i.e., in the air): "since the nature of earthly bodies is able now to bear down on souls sometimes, will not souls also be able to lift earthly bodies upward?"[61]

Thus, resurrection for both Peter Lombard and Hugh of St. Victor is the reassembling of physical body parts to form the spiritual body. Thomas Aquinas, who used both Lombard and Hugh, echoed much of their thinking. In fact, he modeled his *Summa Theologiae* on Lombard's *Sentences*.

Thomas Aquinas

Thomas (1225–74 CE) was born in the kingdom of Naples, and at the age of five his education by Benedictine monks began. Between 1240 and 1243 he entered the Dominican order. He went to Cologne around 1244 where he studied under Albert the Great and was ordained to the priesthood in 1250. He began his public teaching career about 1251–52 at the Dominican Studium in Paris, where he lectured on Peter Lombard's *Sentences*. He was an influential teacher, preacher,

---

[58] Ibid., 2.17.16,19.

[59] Ibid., 2.17.13.

[60] Ibid, 2.17.18. Here, too, Hugh seems to have borrowed from Augustine's *City of God*.

[61] Ibid., 2.17.21.

and writer. Though he wrote many of his works himself, others were written by scribes. He died in 1274 before completing either his *Summa Theologiae* or his *Exposition and Lectures on the Letters of the Apostle Paul*.

The most famous and influential work of Thomas Aquinas is his *Summa Theologiae*, which Reginald of Piperno finished by using Thomas's notes and commentary on Peter Lombard's *Sentences*.[62] This section of the *Summa Theologiae* is referred to today as the *Supplement*, wherein the topic of resurrection is raised in questions 69–86. Thomas discusses matters such as whether the resurrection will be from ashes or whether the ashes from which a human body will be restored has a natural inclination towards its soul.[63] Aquinas cites Augustine (*Enchiridion* 88) as the authority in the *Sed contra* for this same question.

> The human body, although changed into the substance of other bodies or even into its elements, or changed into the food and flesh of human beings and animals, will in an instant return to that human soul which formerly animated it, in order that there might be a living, growing human being.[64]

Thomas argued that the very ashes of a person would be transformed and reunited with the soul of that person to form the resurrected body. Later he said that organic and essential parts most likely would be restored to what they were, though perhaps not accidental parts like hair and nails.[65] Yet, in subsequent questions he stated that hair and nails would rise[66] but things such as sweat, urine, semen, and milk would not.[67]

Thomas addressed the topic of the resurrected body in question 79. He concluded the *respondeo* section of article 1 by writing, "and therefore if it is not the same body which the soul takes back, it will not be called a resurrection, but rather the assumption of a new body."[68] Concluding the *respondeo* section of article 2, he says,

---

[62] Though Reginald finished the work, I shall refer to the author as Thomas Aquinas.

[63] Aquinas, *Supplement*, 78.

[64] Ibid.

[65] Ibid., 79, a. 3, *respondeo*.

[66] Ibid., 80, a. 2, *respondeo*.

[67] Ibid., 80, a. 3, *respondeo*.

[68] Ibid., 79, a. 1, *respondeo*.

> It is necessary that numerically the same person rise again; and this indeed happens when the numerically same soul is united to the numerically same body. For otherwise there would be no resurrection properly speaking, if the same person were not reformed. Hence to claim that the one who will rise is not numerically the same is heretical, since it is contrary to the truth of Scripture, which proclaims the resurrection.[69]

Throughout the discussion of the resurrection in the *Supplement* there is a concern for the physicality of the resurrected body. Questions of age, stature, gender, hair, nails, and movement are all discussed at length.

Besides the *Summa Theologiae*, Thomas also wrote commentaries on the Pauline corpus but died after completing 1 Corinthians 7. Reginald of Piperno finished the commentary, which includes the *lectiones* on chapter 15.[70] One of the primary arguments Aquinas used for the resurrection of the body was that of necessity: "however, the soul, though it be a part of the body of a human being, is not the whole human being, and my soul is not me."[71] Because human beings are body and soul, the body must be raised at the resurrection. He read the four qualities of the resurrected body that Paul mentions in 1 Corinthians 15:42-44 as the gifts (*dotes*) of the resurrected body that flow to it from the soul.[72] The concept of the gifts of the resurrected body became influential in later discussions. Aquinas saw the resurrected body as a physical body.

Second Council of Lyons

In 1274 church officials met at Lyons, France, to discuss, among other matters, the Crusades and the unification of the Eastern and Western Churches. Thomas Aquinas was invited to this council but died on his way there. There were six sessions from May to July of that year. At the fourth session a creed or "symbol of faith" was

---

[69] Ibid., 79, a. 2, *respondeo*.

[70] J. A. Weisheipl, *Friar Thomas D'Aquino: His Life, Thought, and Works* (Washington, DC: Catholic University of America, 1983), 247.

[71] Thomas Aquinas, *Commentary on 1 Corinthians*, chap. 15, lectio 2.

[72] Aquinas, *1 Cor.*, chap. 15, lectio 6. Thomas may have picked up these ideas from earlier scholastics such as Anselm and Eadmer (C. W. Bynum, *The Resurrection of the Body*, 235, n. 21).

read that is now referred to as the "Profession of Faith of Michael Palaeologus." Michael VIII Palaeopogus was the Byzantine Emperor, and although he was not present, his delegation presented the letter, which included a profession of faith from Pope Clement IV (1267), as a creed that could be the basis of unification. The creed itself was not promulgated or even discussed at the council. For our purposes, a key line in the creed reads thus: "We believe also in the true resurrection of this flesh which we now bear."[73]

This formula will be repeated in the new *Catechism* (1994). It goes without saying that in the thirteenth century, church officials did not have a twenty-first century understanding of human biology. However, this simple fact is of profound importance, and we shall return to it later.

Giles of Rome

Giles (b. ca. 1245; d. 1316) was born at Rome between 1243 and 1247. He entered the Hermits of St. Augustine, began his studies in 1260, and completed his master of arts in 1266. It is likely that Giles heard Thomas Aquinas between 1269 and 1272. In 1275 Giles became a Baccalaureus Sententiarus, but was forced to leave his teaching position in Paris in 1279 because of condemnations promulgated by the archbishop of Paris in 1277. The archbishop condemned many positions held by the recently deceased Thomas Aquinas. Giles held positions that were similar to, if not the same as, those condemned by the archbishop.[74] The condemnations are an interesting footnote in the story of a long line of theologians whose positions were condemned during or shortly after their lifetime, only to be endorsed by later church officials. Giles eventually returned to his teaching post, and in

---

[73] *Credimus etiam veram resurrectionem huius carnis, quam nunc gestamus,* DS 854.

[74] Of the many positions condemned in 1277, two had to do with resurrection. The first condemned anyone who would deny the numerical identity of the risen body with the mortal body. The second condemned anyone who would deny that the resurrection was demonstrable philosophically. Giles held neither of these two opinions. K. Nolan, *The Immortality of the Soul and the Resurrection of the Body according to Giles of Rome: A Historical Study of a Thirteenth Century Theological Problem,* SEAug 7, no. 1 (Rome: Studium Theologicum Augustinianum, 1967), 67.

1287 his order declared his teachings to be its official teachings. Giles became general of the Order in 1292, and archbishop of Bourges in 1295. He died in 1316. Giles also wrote a commentary on Lombard's *Sentences* but never finished it. Because the commentary ends before the fourth book, he did not address per se the eschatological questions contained therein.[75] He did write *Quaestiones de resurrectione mortuorum*, which K. Nolan has reproduced.[76]

Giles maintained that the soul survived after death. He believed that although the soul is naturally mortal, it is supernaturally immortal. Giles understood the soul as the form of the body (*forma corporis*):

> Therefore the rational soul, which is the form of the body, does not have being in itself, because no form while it is form has being in itself. Rather, it has being in its matter. And it does not act by itself, because the soul does not understand, but a human being acts by the soul.[77]

As such, the soul is responsible for the numerical identity of a person.

Giles addressed the question whether all the food a person ate during the course of his life would be raised in the resurrected body. The underlying question was really one of organic change, as it was for Methodius a millennium before. Giles entertained a number of different opinions regarding the nature of organic change, food, and the human body, but eventually claimed that numerical identity is retained by the soul of a person, not the body. Giles recognized that the body changes throughout life, while that person's soul remains the same "so as long as an individual lives, so long the same soul and the same form remain, because the flesh changes according to its matter; that soul or form exists at times in more, at times in less, matter."[78]

Giles believed that since soul and body were essential characteristics of the human being, the resurrection was logical. The immortality Adam experienced before sin was the immortality human beings would experience at the resurrection. Whether God would use the material from an earthly body to form the resurrected body is known

---

[75] Ibid., 114, n. 2.

[76] Ibid. There is no critical edition of *Quaestiones de resurrectione mortuorum*.

[77] Giles of Rome, *Sent.*, III, d. 1 p. 1 q. 1 a. 2 11 B, cited in Nolan, *Immortality*, 59 n. 46.

[78] Giles of Rome, *Quaestiones*, in Nolan, *Immortality*, 110.

only to God. Giles did not think it necessary, however, for the earthly matter of our bodies of flesh to be the basis for our resurrected bodies. He believed the resurrection to be the reconstitution of the person, not merely the awakening of the body.

Thus, the scholastics generally understood the resurrection in physical terms and followed the thinking of Augustine. The resurrection itself was logical, as a human being was understood to be both body and soul. How God formed the resurrected body was open to debate, though they insisted that the resurrected body would be material and the human would be whole.[79]

The teaching of the scholastic period is summarized in one line of the Second General Council of Lyons (1274): "we believe also in the true resurrection of this flesh which we now bear."[80]

Reformation

The nature of the resurrected body was not a battleground during the Reformation. As such, there were not many foundational discussions about it. When the resurrection was addressed, there was a general reaffirmation of Augustinian teachings concerning the nature of the resurrection and the resurrection body.

Martin Luther

Martin Luther (1483–1546 CE) was born in Eisleben, Germany. In 1505 he entered the Augustinian monastery at Erfurt and was ordained a priest in 1507. He was sent to Wittenberg during the winter of 1508–9. Ten years after his ordination he affixed his ninety-five theses to the door of the castle church at Wittenberg. The *Augsburg Confession* was written by his follower, P. Melanchthon, in 1530. In 1534, after twelve years of work, Luther finished his German translation of the Bible. The Council of Trent was called in 1544 in response to the Reformation and concluded in December 1563. Luther died where he was born — in Eisleben.

Of Luther's many works addressing resurrection (such as in both the greater and small catechism and various homilies), there exists a commentary on 1 Corinthians 15, in which Luther envisioned the

---

[79] See also C. W. Bynum, *The Resurrection of the Body*, 265.
[80] DS, 854.

resurrected body in a physical way. He retained patristic images and arguments by saying that God was capable of reassembling body parts that had been strewn across the world. He also postulated characteristics of the spiritual body.

> But it will be a spiritual body, not because it lacks flesh and blood, but because it will not require bodily necessities, but life springs from looking at God and from the soul. Afterward in the body, I will hear and I will see over a hundred thousand miles and all knuckles, flesh, bones — but in another form. As now stars in heaven do not need a warm room, eating, drinking, sleeping, waking, as we do. Nevertheless they are celestial bodies, but they do not need bodily necessities, as we do.[81]

Indeed Luther said, "No, Paul, I am speaking clearly. It is to be a spiritual body, what at first led a natural and animal existence, shall become spiritual."[82] The resurrected body meant, for Luther, a body that has life but no need to eat, sleep, or digest.

> There it will not be so; you will not eat, you will not sleep, digest, or defecate, or take a wife, or bake or brew. That is natural existence now on earth. This is said about the soul or bodily life, perishable life. The body lives with five senses; it must reproduce itself and nourish itself, but not there; it will not be such a life, but [will be] a spiritual body. Not as heretics and fools who used to say, "We shall not have a body there, because he says 'spiritual.'" But it will live by the spirit; the belly will live, even if it does not have food; it will not need a bed or the necessities of this life. But God will be "all in all."[83]

Luther spoke of a physical resurrected body. "There will be a face, eyes, nose, belly, leg, arm — these it will be. But spiritual [parts], that is, not animal (parts), as here to eat, drink, and digest. That will cease there."[84]

The spiritual body will be the object of angels' sung praises and admiring smiles "angels will marvel at the beauty of fingers."[85] Luther

---

[81] Martin Luther, *Commentary on 1 Corinthians*, ed. A. Leitzmann and O. Clemen, *Luthers Werke in Auswahl* 7 (Berlin: W. de Gruyter, 1962), 341.

[82] Ibid., 343.

[83] Ibid., 340.

[84] Ibid.

[85] Ibid., 339.

then did not so much add new speculative knowledge to the nature of the resurrected body as he did present it in imaginative and vivid terms.

The Roman Catechism

The final session of the Council of Trent (1563) decreed that an official catechism of the Catholic Church be published. Pope Pius IV appointed Cardinal Charles Borromeo as president of the commission; three years later, the Roman Catechism was printed and promulgated. It is divided into four parts: the Apostles' Creed, Sacraments, the Ten Commandments, and Prayer (the Our Father).

The catechism addressed the resurrection in the first part, which dealt with the Apostles' Creed. The eleventh article of the creed states, "I believe in the resurrection of the flesh (*carnis resurrectionem*)."[86] This is not the language of the New Testament but that of a later creed. In retaining creedal language, the catechism perpetuated the notion of the resurrected body of flesh that had been understood since at least the second century.

The catechism also addressed the question of terminology, asking "why the apostles called the resurrection of mankind 'the resurrection of the flesh.'"[87] It answered that the apostles wished to show the immortality of the soul. The soul does not need to be raised, but the flesh does. By limiting the language to resurrection of the flesh, the apostles indicated that the soul lives eternally.[88]

The catechism stated plainly that the identical and same body will rise,[89] though the bodies of the blessed will possess *ornamenta*, the chief of which are the four gifts (*dotes*) of *impassibilitas, claritas, agilitas,* and *subtilitas*.[90] The catechism reinforced earlier teachings on the resurrected body by retaining the theological parlance of the day, used to convey concepts not present in the Pauline passage of 1 Corinthians 15:42-44. The catechism explained that *impassibilitas* allowed the risen body to

---

[86] *Catechismus ex Decreto Concilii Tridentini ad Parochos* (Rome: Societas S. Joannis Evangelistae; Tournai: Desclée, 1902), 95.

[87] *Catechismus*, 95.

[88] Ibid.

[89] Ibid., 99.

[90] Ibid., 101–3.

suffer nothing, neither heat nor cold, neither pain nor inconvenience. Of course, this is a gift not given to the damned, for they would feel and experience pain. *Claritas* is a gift by which the blessed shall "shine like the sun."[91] This gift is not given to each in the same degree; some will shine more brightly. The catechism used 1 Corinthians 15:41-42 to prove the point.[92] The third gift is *agilitas*, by which the resurrected body can move freely, with ease and without inhibition.[93] The fourth gift, *subtilitas*, allows the body to be completely subservient to the soul.

The catechism thus did not forge new ground in resurrection theology. Rather, it summarized the teachings of the day, which had been heavily influenced by creeds, church fathers, and other theologians. As the Reformation was not concerned primarily with the resurrection, it is not surprising that Luther and the Council of Trent expressed similar ideas concerning it. Both were influenced by the terminology *resurrectionem carnis* and *dotes*—concepts foreign to Paul and other New Testament writers.

Recent Scholarship and Statements

In the past century we have witnessed the Catholic Church embrace critical study of the Bible and historical theology. The fruits of this research have recast earlier positions in contemporary language, while at the same time upholding authentic Christian faith. This process has not been without some controversy. The following material will show how the discussion about resurrection has changed in the past one hundred years.

Early Twentieth Century

Much of the first half of the twentieth century saw a ratification of earlier expressions and terminology for the resurrected body as a physical body. A small number of Catholic commentators are cited herein as examples of such literature.

---

[91] "*Hanc consequitur claritas, qua sanctorum corpora tamquam sol fulgebunt*" (ibid., 102).

[92] Ibid., 102.

[93] The catechism cites Augustine, *City of God*, 13.18, 20; 22.11 and Jerome's commentary on Isaiah (40).

Joseph MacRory (1861–1945)

MacRory, archbishop of Armagh and professor of Scripture and Oriental Languages at Maynooth, published a commentary on 1 Corinthians that parroted much of the traditional theological teachings concerning the resurrected body. He maintained that the very body laid in the tomb is raised. MacRory acknowledged three qualities of the resurrected body: *impassibilitas*, *claritas*, and *agilitas*. In speaking of the traditionally understood fourth gift, *subtilitas*, MacRory saw that that "spiritual" aspect encompassed the three other qualities and expressed in one word the condition of the resurrected body. Yet MacRory maintained that it is a spiritual body, "not in the sense that it will cease to be material (Luke 24:39), or that it will be composed of air or ether or light, for it will be the same body that went into the grave, and hence of the same nature, though transformed we cannot say how much."[94] Although he admitted that "spiritual" is not so much a quality of the resurrected body as an apt term to express its condition, he did not break new ground.

Charles Callan (1877–1962)

The Dominican Father Callan also retained the concept of gifts or qualities of the resurrected body. In his commentary on 1 Corinthians, he juxtaposed the natural body — imperfect, tiring, slow to respond to the soul, requiring food and rest — with the spiritual body — gifted with *agilitas*, strong, "perfectly united to the soul."[95] In addressing the adjective "spiritual" as applied to the resurrected body, Callan said that it is "entirely subject to the needs and wishes of the glorified soul. This does not mean that the risen body ceases to be material, but that it is freed from those conditions and functions which serve only a temporal end and which make it the imperfect instrument of the glorified spirit."[96]

---

[94] J. MacRory, *The Epistles of St. Paul to the Corinthians*, vol. 2 (St. Louis: B. Herder, 1915), 246.

[95] C. Callan, *The Epistles of Paul: 1. Romans, First and Second Corinthians, Galatians* (New York: Wagner, 1922), 431.

[96] Ibid., 431.

Henry Leighton Goudge (1866–1939)

The fifth revised edition of Goudge's commentary on 1 Corinthians appeared in 1926. In it, Goudge, like other commentators before him, read Paul's statements about resurrection and the resurrected body with an eye to the appearance stories in the gospels—a tendency cited as a factor leading to the belief in resurrection of the flesh.[97] Goudge spelled out well the relationship he believed was at work between the Pauline letters and the appearance stories in the gospel accounts. He telescoped these traditions into one, when he stated that the gospel narratives

> represent the body of the Risen Lord, just as S. Paul does. On the one hand, He has a real body, and is not merely a glorious spirit (Luke 24:39, 40; see also 1 Cor 15:44); on the other hand, that body has been raised in incorruption, glory and power; it is no longer under bondage to the laws of space (John 20:19); our Lord in His Whole Person has become "spirit" (Luke 24:31), and spirit that quickens those to whom He communicates Himself (John 20:22). Now the agreement of S. Paul with the Gospel narratives is a strong argument for their truth.[98]

Of course, exegesis has changed since the early twentieth century. No longer is it acceptable to read all New Testament accounts through a singular lens that blurs any real or substantial theological difference. The lens of critical scholarship has allowed us to recognize different priorities, emphases, and even theologies present in the various works that comprise the New Testament. This recognition allows the modern reader to analyze and to respect the differences of each author rather than to blend them together into one homogenized theology, though it may be a real temptation.

Rudolf Bultmann (1884–1976)

The Lutheran biblical scholar Rudolf Bultmann broke with traditional categories of scriptural interpretation and stressed the need

[97] J. G. Davies, "Factors Leading to the Emergence of Belief in the Resurrection of the Flesh," *JTS* 23 (1972): 448–55.

[98] H. Goudge, *The First Epistle to the Corinthians*, 5th rev. ed. (London, 1926), 158.

to demythologize the New Testament by preaching in language that would assist individuals in making a decision for or against Christ. He saw that much of the language and stories of the New Testament were difficult for modern people to accept. For example, he found resurrection from the dead, and miracles in general, basically meaningless.

With respect to the topic of the resurrected body, Bultmann cast aside the traditional concept of *dotes* and chose instead to speak of a spiritual body as a "Spirit-ruled *soma*."[99] He argued to this point by showing that a person "as a whole, can be denoted by *soma*."[100] Thus, Bultmann claimed that Paul's concept of the self was not shaped by a Hellenistic dualism distinguishing sharply between the *sōma* and the *psychē*, though at times he comes close to expressing that view.[101] The *sōma* referred to a human being as human, while *sarx* referred to a power that laid claim to the person. "That is why Paul can speak of a life *kata sarka* (according to the flesh) but never of a life *kata sōma* (according to the body)."[102] Thus at the resurrection, Bultmann maintained that the *sōma*, rather than reconstituted flesh, would be transformed so as to be no longer under the power of the flesh but ruled by the Spirit (i.e., more akin to a renewed personality than a renewed physique).

By disregarding previous discussion on the qualities of the resurrected body and retaining biblical language, Bultmann added a new dimension to the discussion. In some sense, it was no longer necessary even to maintain that anything physical would be raised. Bultmann caused tremendous reaction, both positive and negative.[103] All scholars

---

[99] R. Bultmann, *Theology of the New Testament*, vol. 1 (London: SCM Press, 1952–55), 201.

[100] Ibid., 195.

[101] Ibid., 201–2.

[102] Ibid., 201.

[103] Many scholars rejected Bultmann's demythologizing the resurrection altogether in favor of a physical resurrection. Conservative Protestant scholars such as Grosheide and Schep (one of Grosheide's students) maintained a belief in a fleshly resurrection. Schep stated plainly that "the resurrection body will consist of glorified flesh." *The Nature of the Resurrection Body* (Grand Rapids, MI: Eerdmans, 1964), 184. He based his arguments on early creeds that purport to be the teaching of the apostles, and on early church fathers who taught the resurrection of the flesh based on the resurrected Christ.

in the latter half of the twentieth century commenting on the resurrected body responded to Bultmann either directly or indirectly.

For example, E. P. Sanders also seems to have grappled with Paul's intent, and he admitted that it is difficult to say what transformation and change would be like. Paul had seen the risen Lord, and there had been a transformation. Rather than a ghost, Christ is the first fruits of the resurrection. The resurrected body is not natural but spiritual, and still there is some connection between the ordinary and the resurrected person.[104]

Karl Rahner, a systematic theologian rather than a biblical scholar, recognized the inadequacy of language to express resurrection.

> In the last analysis, therefore, we can merely say in Saint Paul's language of paradox: it will be a spiritual body (1 Cor 15:44), i.e., a true bodily nature which, however, is pure expression of the Spirit become one with the pneuma of God and its bodily existence, and is no longer its restricting and abasing element and its emptiness. It will be a bodily nature which does not cancel again the freedom from the earthly here-and-now gained with death, but will, on the contrary, bring it out in its pure form.[105]

Joseph Ratzinger too, in his influential *Introduction to Christianity*, states: "One thing at any rate may be fairly clear: both John (6:53) and Paul (1 Cor 15:50) state with all possible emphasis that the 'resurrection of the flesh,' the 'resurrection of the body' is not a 'resurrection of physical bodies.'"[106] Ratzinger summarizes with a question to which the reply is affirmative:

> To recapitulate, Paul teaches not the resurrection of physical bodies but the resurrection of persons, and this not in the return of the "fleshly body," that is, the biological structure, an idea which he expressly describes as impossible ("the perishable cannot become imperishable"), but in the different form of the life of the resurrection, as shown in the risen Lord?[107]

---

[104] E. P. Sanders, *Paul* (Oxford: Oxford University, 1991), 29.

[105] K. Rahner, "The Resurrection of the Body," in *Theological Investigations 2: Man in the Church* (Baltimore: Helicon, 1963), 214.

[106] J. Ratzinger, *Introduction to Christianity*, trans. J. R. Foster (New York, NY: Herder and Herder, 1971), 277.

[107] Ibid.

Thus, more recent Catholic theologians seem to have recognized the inadequacy of grossly physical language to speak of the resurrection of the dead. The language used by these influential Catholic scholars was consistent with language used by the Second Vatican Council.

Official (Recent) Church Teaching

For the most part, Catholic scholars in the early twentieth century reiterated traditional church teaching, albeit with slight modifications. The Lutheran scholar Bultmann leapfrogged the discussion of the physical, resurrected body by stating that the spiritual body would be a spirit-ruled *sōma*. His position caused a wide variety of responses, perhaps even including the Vatican II fathers who used pastoral language to express the faith of the church and, at times, used new terminology in addition to citing older decrees.[108] Significantly, Vatican II never explicitly repeats the phrase "resurrection of the flesh" or even "resurrection of the body." Instead, in the Pastoral Constitution on the Church in the Modern World (*Gaudium et Spes*) we read:

> We do not know the moment of the consummation of the earth and of humanity nor the way the universe will be transformed. The form of this world, distorted by sin, is passing away and we are taught that God is preparing a new dwelling and a new earth in which righteousness dwells, whose happiness will fill and surpass all the desires of peace arising in human hearts. Then death will have been conquered, the daughters and sons of God will be raised in Christ and what was sown in weakness and dishonor will become incorruptible; charity and its works will remain and all of creation, which God made for humanity, will be set free from its bondage to decay.[109]

---

[108] "This sacred council accepts loyally the venerable faith of our ancestors in the living communion which exists between us and our sisters and brothers who are in the glory of heaven or who are yet being purified after their death; and it reiterates the decrees of the Second Council of Nicea, the Council of Florence, and the Council of Trent" (LG 51). See next note for full citation.

[109] *Gaudium et Spes* 39 in Austin Flannery, ed., *Vatican Council II: The Basic Sixteen Documents* (Northport, NY: Costello Publishing Co., 1996). All references to Vatican II documents are from this edition.

The language is scriptural and traditional without being to\ descriptive. Though earlier in the same document the Vatican fathers are sure to proclaim that "the human person, though made of body and soul, is a unity" (GS 14), four paragraphs later they admit:

> It is when faced with death that the enigma of the human condition is most evident. . . . Because they [men and women] bear in themselves the seed of eternity, which cannot be reduced to mere matter, they rebel against death. . . . For God has called men and women, and still calls them, to attach themselves with all their being to him in sharing for ever a life that is divine and free from all decay. Christ won this victory when he rose to life, for by his death he freed women and men from death. Faith, therefore, with its solidly based teaching, provides thoughtful people with an answer to their anxious queries about their future lot. At the same time it makes them capable of being united in Christ with their loved ones who have already died, and gives hope that they have found true life with God. (GS 18)

Thus the pastoral constitution retains body and soul language, but does so in a way as to preserve human unity. In so doing, the constitution does not give us physical descriptions of the resurrected life but instead speaks in more amorphous terms about humanity sharing a divine life free from decay. After the council, Catholic theologians addressed many questions about resurrection, including the "when."[110]

Shortly after the election of Archbishop Karol Wotyla as Pope John Paul II, the Congregation for the Doctrine of the Faith published the *Letter on Certain Questions Concerning Eschatology (LCQCE)*. One purpose of the letter was to address the doubt that was "gradually insinuating itself deeply into people's minds." The CDF thought

---

[110] Broadly speaking, Karl Rahner represents a school of thought that would see resurrection happening at the moment of one's death. At death, one is no longer bound by time and space but immediately enters into eternity and, therefore, resurrected life. A different school of thought is represented by Joseph Ratzinger, now Pope Emeritus Benedict XVI, who maintains the traditional view that a personal resurrection is concurrent with the general resurrection / last judgment. As prefect of the Congregation for the Doctrine of the Faith, Ratzinger had the opportunity to articulate this understanding from a different vantage point.

\n would avoid thinking about life after death when
ions such as: "Is there really anything after death?
__main of us when we die? Is it nothingness that is
_s?" The Congregation notes that these questions have arisen
because of the work of theologians, "the precise subject and the significance of which is beyond the discernment of the majority of the
faithful. . . . since they no longer find the vocabulary they are used
to and their familiar ideas." The letter goes on to state that its intent
is not to restrict theological inquiry, which is both necessary and
profitable, but to safeguard faith. The letter, then, enumerates seven
points of church teaching regarding eschatology, the first three of
which are reproduced here:

1. The Church believes (cf. the Creed) in the resurrection of the
   dead.
2. The Church understands this resurrection as referring to *the
   whole person*; for the elect it is nothing other than the extension
   to human beings of the resurrection of Christ himself.
3. The Church affirms that a spiritual element survives and subsists after death, an element endowed with consciousness and
   will, so that the "human self" subsists. To designate this element, the Church uses the word "soul," the accepted term in
   the usage of Scripture and Tradition. Although not unaware
   that this term has various meanings in the Bible, the Church
   thinks that there is no valid reason for rejecting it; moreover, she
   considers that the use of some word as a vehicle is absolutely
   indispensable in order to support the faith of Christians.[111]

In concluding, the letter states that "neither Scripture nor theology
provides sufficient light for a proper picture of life after death. . . .
We must . . . be firm with regard to the essence of the doctrine and
at the same time careful not to allow childish or arbitrary images to
be considered truths of faith."[112] Also important is the recognition
that a "spiritual element," "the human self," endures after death. The
church uses the term "soul" to designate this element. This definition
of "soul" is markedly different from Plato, Aristotle, or even Tatian's

[111] *LCQCE.*
[112] *LCQCE.*

notion.[113] To speak of the soul as the human self opens new doors of understanding for the modern Christian.

This important letter seems as relevant today as it was more than thirty years ago. The letter seemed to have opened the door slightly to the possibility of recognizing that the term "body" can be understood in a way more broadly than "flesh." The letter, however, did not halt all of the controversy or inquiry surrounding this issue. For only four short years later another document from the Congregation for the Doctrine of the Faith was promulgated. This time, however, there was a different prefect. Cardinal Seper had retired and Cardinal Ratzinger had taken the reins. The short missive issued in December of 1983 made clear that the church understood "resurrection of the dead" and "resurrection of the flesh" to be "diverse and complementary expressions of the same primitive tradition of the Church." There was a stated desire to return to the literal translation of the Latin term *resurrectionem carnis*. The brief note also makes clear that

> the abandonment of the formula "resurrection of the flesh" has the danger of supporting current theories that place the resurrection at the moment of death, excluding in practice the bodily resurrection, especially of *this* flesh. On the diffusion today of such a vision "spiritualizing" the resurrection, the Sacred Congregation for the Doctrine of the Faith has attracted the attention of the bishops in its letter "On Certain Questions Concerning Eschatology" of May 17, 1979.[114]

The door that had been opened slightly in 1979 seemed to close again. By emphasizing "*this* flesh," the CDF seemed to encourage a more literal understanding of resurrection. Though Cardinal Ratzinger had written in 1971 that Paul was not teaching the return of fleshly bodies with their biological structures, the emphasis in 1983 on a resurrection of *this* flesh represents a shift in thinking.

Less than ten years after this clarification from Cardinal Ratzinger's CDF, the first edition of the new *Catechism* was published,

---

[113] Plato, *Phaedr.*, 246c; Aristotle, *De An.* 2.1. 413a; Tatian, *Address to the Greeks*, 15.

[114] See appendix C for the official French and the author's own English translations.

repeating the formula from Trent, which itself is a restatement of the Second Council of Lyons: "We believe in the true resurrection of this flesh that we now possess" (CCC 1017). This statement appears in the new *Catechism* in the section on the creed, in particular in the section on the article: "I Believe in the Resurrection of the Body." The tendency to retain traditional language, even if it is laden with philosophical presuppositions not shared with the modern world, is exemplified in this article. Yet, in the same section, under the article "On the Third Day He Rose Again from the Dead," the church teaches:

> Christ's Resurrection was not a return to earthly life, as was the case with the raisings from the dead that he had performed before Easter: Jairus' daughter, the young man of Naim, Lazarus. These actions were miraculous events, but the persons miraculously raised returned by Jesus' power to ordinary earthly life. At some particular moment they would die again. Christ's Resurrection is essentially different. In his risen body he passes from the state of death to another life beyond time and space. At Jesus' Resurrection his body is filled with the power of the Holy Spirit: he shares the divine life in his glorious state, so that St. Paul can say that Christ is "the man of heaven." (CCC 646; cf. 1 Cor 15:35-50)

Important phrases in this paragraph are the recognition that "Christ's Resurrection is essentially different. In his risen body he passes from the state of death to another life beyond time and space." It seems the church has retained the language from Lyons in paragraph 1017 while at the same time forging new, more modern expressions in paragraph 646.

Finally, Pope John Paul II himself chose to address some of these eschatological questions when he delivered three general audiences in the summer of 1999. In these talks, he spoke of heaven, hell, and purgatory in personalist terms. For example, he said:

> In the context of Revelation, we know that the "heaven" or "happiness" in which we will find ourselves is neither an abstraction nor a physical place in the clouds, but a living, personal relationship with the Holy Trinity. It is our meeting with the Father which takes place in the risen Christ through the communion of the Holy Spirit.
>
> It is always necessary to maintain a certain restraint in describing these "ultimate realities" since their depiction is always unsatisfactory. Today, personalist language is better suited to

describing the state of happiness and peace we will enjoy in our definitive communion with God.[115]

Coupled with this personalist language is the traditional teaching of the human being as body and soul. We saw how Vatican II preserved this traditional teaching in *Gaudium et Spes*, paragraph 14. That notion of body and soul is carried into the United States Catholic Catechism for Adults when it claims that "not only do our souls survive physical death, but even our bodies will rise again at the end of time at the Last Judgment and resurrection of the dead."[116]

When faced with such a graphic, physical, fleshly notion of resurrection, many modern Christians may ask, along with the Corinthians, "How are the dead raised? With what sort of body do they come?" (1 Cor 15:35). It will be good to remind ourselves that Paul's initial answer to the Corinthians was "Fool!" (1 Cor 15:36). He ultimately concluded by saying that if a physical body is sown, a spiritual body is raised, for flesh and blood shall not inherit the kingdom of God (1 Cor 15:44, 50).

The early church was faced with a number of theological issues from inside and outside the community. One such issue that commanded attention was resurrection. Though Paul seems to have imagined a life with Christ that transcended physical notions of flesh and blood, the early church quickly fell into a position of defending a resurrection of the flesh. Jerome and Augustine solidified ideas of earlier theologians in staunchly proclaiming a fleshy resurrection. Medieval scholastic thinking, for the most part, echoed Jerome and Augustine. The Council of Trent codified the church's understanding of belief in the resurrection of the flesh, claiming that the apostles deliberately used the term "resurrection of the flesh" to teach the immortality of the soul. Bultmann represented the existential response to the resurrection by claiming that the spiritual body was a "Spirit-ruled *sōma*." Even though Vatican II may have breathed fresh air into the matter for Catholics by avoiding graphic, physical language for the afterlife, more recent Catholic teaching, as articulated in the catechism, has served to repeat these claims from Trent and earlier times. The result may be that the church has retained language not well suited for the

---

[115] General Audience, July 21, 1999.
[116] *USCCA*, p. 93.

modern world. By hearing both "resurrection of this flesh" and "a life beyond time and space" to speak of resurrection, the modern person may be confused. It might behoove the modern Christian to peel away the layers of philosophical categories, doctrinal statements, and the history of theology to recover a New Testament understanding of resurrection. What did the early Christians mean by the term and why did they apply it to Jesus?

Chapter 2

Biblical Data

Resurrection from the Dead → ~~document~~ appears in NT not *res. of body*

A reexamination of the biblical text would serve us well at this point. By doing so we find that neither "resurrection of the flesh" (*anastasis sarkos*) nor "resurrection of the body" (*anastasis sōmatos*) appears in the New Testament. Church fathers introduced each of those terms. Instead, in the New Testament one finds the term "resurrection of the dead" (*anastasis nekrōn*).[1] Or even as some would translate: resurrection "from/out of the dead ones" (*ek [tōn] nekrōn*).[2] Why the language shifted from "resurrection from/of the dead" to "resurrection of the flesh/body" has been the subject of some debate, which we will not engage here.[3] Even though the "resurrection of the flesh" and even "resurrection of the body" is not found in the New Testament, the terms continue to be used to the present day.

Old Testament

Anthropological Presuppositions

Most of the biblical tradition does not posit a body-soul anthropology.[4] The Bible was not written as a text about philosophy but

---

[1] E.g., Matt 22:31; Luke 20:35; Acts 4:2; 17:32; 23:6; 24:21; 26:23; Rom 1:4; 1 Cor 15:12, 13, 21, 42; Heb 6:2; 1 Pet 1:3.

[2] E.g., 1 Thess 1:10; see also Eph 5:14.

[3] E.g., J. G. Davies, "Factors Leading to the Emergence of Belief in the Resurrection of the Flesh," *JTS* 23 (1972): 448–55 and Brian Schmisek, "Augustine's Use of 'Spiritual Body,'" *AugSt* 35:2 (2004): 237–52.

[4] One later Jewish book was heavily influenced by Greek thought. The book of Wisdom (The Wisdom of Solomon), composed in Greek around the first century BCE in Alexandrian Egypt, accepts some concepts in Greek philosophy and recasts them in the light of Jewish faith. For example, the book of Wisdom borrowed the Greek idea of the immortal soul to say that

primarily as a text about God, and the people's interaction with him. "Soul" is a Greek notion not found often in the Bible, especially not in the Old Testament.

Rather than a single unified anthropology, the Old Testament displays varied anthropological presuppositions. Even so, we are able to say that an Old Testament anthropology generally sees the human being as a unified whole, not as Plato would have it. The unified human being had different aspects such as "blood," "breath," "heart," "spirit," "being," or "flesh."[5] These aspects were not always clearly delineated. The term *bāsār* (flesh) expresses the physical aspect of human life, the human being in its weakness, and in its relation to all animal life. The term *nephesh* (being) formulates the living or vital

---

when the righteous die, their souls are with God. For even if the righteous are not rewarded in this life, they will receive their reward in the next because "justice is undying" (Wis 1:15). The concept of the "souls of the righteous" being "in the hand of God" was heretofore unknown in biblical literature.

> The souls of the righteous are in the hand of God, and no torment shall touch them. They seemed, in the view of the foolish, to be dead; and their passing away was thought an affliction and their going forth from us, utter destruction. But they are in peace. For if to others, indeed, they seem punished, yet is their hope full of immortality; Chastised a little, they shall be greatly blessed, because God tried them and found them worthy of himself. As gold in the furnace, he proved them, and as sacrificial offerings he took them to himself. In the time of their judgment they shall shine and dart about as sparks through stubble; They shall judge nations and rule over peoples, and the LORD shall be their King forever. Those who trust in him shall understand truth, and the faithful shall abide with him in love: Because grace and mercy are with his holy ones, and his care is with the elect. (Wis 3:1-9, NABRE)

The passage cited above is often used at Catholic funeral liturgies today, though the language of "souls of the just" may be more familiar, as that was the translation used the past forty years before it was recently changed to "souls of the righteous." To many, it is a comforting thought that the souls of the just are with God. It should be noted that the book of Wisdom is deuterocanonical and therefore not read in Protestant churches. "Average Catholics" are more familiar with this book than "average Protestants" or even "average Jews."

[5] Each of these underlying Hebrew terms ("flesh" *bāsār*, "being" *nephesh*, "spirit" *rûāh*, "heart" *leb*, "breath" *něshāmāh*, and "blood" *dam*) is translated by a number of Greek terms in the LXX.

aspect of a being, whereas *rūăh* (spirit) expresses its inner disposition and ability to be moved by God. Each of these terms individually can express the human being as a whole.

Moreover, when the Hebrew Scriptures were translated into Greek (this translation is referred to as the Septuagint, abbreviated as LXX), the translation of Hebrew terms was not always a one-to-one correspondence — that is, not every instance of the Hebrew term *bāsār* (flesh) was translated by the Greek term *sarx* (flesh). Thus, unclear Hebrew anthropological aspects, which were not clearly delineated in the Hebrew language, were further complicated by a Greek translation. Indeed, Greek introduced a term foreign to Hebrew: *sōma* (body). Although Hebrew anthropological terms are often translated into Greek or English with a one-to-one correspondence (e.g., the Hebrew *nephesh* is often rendered in Greek as *psychē* and in English as "soul"), such translations, at times, do violence to the underlying philosophical and anthropological presuppositions of the languages. Recognizing these varied Old Testament anthropological presuppositions and how they influence the LXX and the New Testament is critical to a better understanding of resurrection.

Even though the New Testament was written in Greek, the majority of it echoes the sentiments of the Old Testament more than it echoes Greek philosophy. That is, we will be misguided if we read the New Testament with Platonic or Aristotelian lenses rather than Old Testament lenses. For example, the New Testament, like the Old Testament, presupposes the human being as a unity rather than a composite of body and soul.

So for the biblical authors, the human being is most often understood as an indivisible whole and not, as Plato would have it, divided into *sōma* and *psychē*. Yet the human being has many aspects including thoughts, feelings, desires, moral weakness, and receptivity to the action of God. Despite this biblical data, and despite our living in the modern world in which biology and scientific inquiry enhance or even replace philosophical speculation about the human body and soul, most modern Christians tend to think of the human being in terms of Platonic philosophy: mortal body and immortal soul.

Old Testament Texts: Life after Death

Various thoughts and beliefs about afterlife percolated throughout the ancient world. Resurrection as a particular belief about afterlife was generally denied in the Greek world: "but when the dust has drawn up the blood of a man, once he is dead, there is no resurrection."[6]

The most important matter for our discussion is the notion of life after death found in the Old Testament. Most of the Old Testament authors recognized that once a living thing dies, it goes to the grave (Ps 89:48; Isa 38:18; Ezek 28:2; 31:14) with no hope of an afterlife (Job 7:9; 10:21-22; 14:10-12; Pss 6:5; 30:10; 88:11-13; Prov 2:18-19). Though most of the Old Testament shows no awareness of a life after death, some passages do indicate this as a possibility. For example, some scholars see Isaiah 53:10-12 as reflecting a hope for the Servant of Yahweh to triumph over death, in as much as it says that the Lord will allot him a portion with the great.[7] Others see Isaiah 25:8 as expressing a hope for afterlife in that the LORD[8] of hosts will "destroy death forever" (NABRE). Another difficult passage from the same book is Isaiah 26:19, but the Hebrew is unclear (we will explore this passage in more detail below). In the end, the book of Isaiah does not have a clear expression of life after death, and at least one passage argues against it: "For it is not Sheol that gives you thanks, nor death that praises you; Neither do those who go down into the pit await your kindness" (Isa 38:18; NABRE). Psalm 6:6 echoes Isaiah 38:18: "For in death there is no remembrance of you. Who praises you in Sheol?" (NABRE). But certain psalms do grope with the possibility of life after death. Though both Psalm 49 (esp. v. 15) and Psalm 73 (vv. 24–28) lament the fact that all human beings die, the author of each psalm expresses hope that Yahweh will deliver him from death. Exactly what this deliverance is would be difficult to articulate, for only a vague hope is expressed (Pss 49:15; 73:24-28).

What about Resurrection in OT?

Resurrection in the Old Testament

The passages treated thus far speak vaguely of life after death. What about resurrection? When does that idea originate? We might be surprised to learn that in the Old Testament, other than an occa-

---

[6] Aeschylus, *Eum.*, 647–48. Cf. Homer, *Il.*, 24.551; Herodotus, 3.62.4; Aeschylus, *Ag.* 1360; Sophocles, *El.*, 137.

[7] *NJBC*, 1314.

[8] When the English term "LORD" appears in a biblical translation in small capitals, as it does here, it designates the underlying Hebrew term YHWH, which is also known as the tetragrammaton (the four-lettered name of God).

sional story of a prophet raising the dead (e.g., 1 Kgs 17:17-24; 2 Kgs 4:18-37), there is little mention of resurrection and what is there is fairly late: Isaiah 26:19, Job 19:26, Daniel 12:2-3, and 2 Maccabees 7.

Isaiah 26:19 is a difficult case in that the Hebrew is unclear. Even so, the Greek version states:

> The dead shall be raised [*anastēsontai*] and those in the graves
>   shall rise [*egerthēsontai*];
> those in the land shall rejoice, for your dew is radiant for them.
> The land of the godless will be destroyed. (translation mine)

The significance of the Greek version lies in the words for raised (*anistēmi*) and rise (*egeirō*). Both Greek verbs have a wide semantic range that includes extensive use in the New Testament to refer to Jesus (and others) being raised from the dead. So even though the Hebrew is unclear, the Greek translation of it seems to be clear. The first part of the verse uses parallelism, a device whereby the author says fundamentally the same thing twice, using slightly different images. Here, "the dead shall be raised" is roughly synonymous with "those in the graves shall rise." same

The book of Job, particularly 19:26b, is often cited as demonstrating a belief in resurrection:

> As for me, I know that my vindicator lives,
> and that he will at last stand forth upon the dust.
> This will happen when my skin has been stripped off,
> and from my flesh I will see God. (Job 19:25-26; NABRE)

Job

However, like the Isaiah passage above, the verse from Job is riddled with difficulties. As M. Pope noted in his commentary on Job years ago, "the verse is notoriously difficult. The ancient versions all differ and no reliance can be placed in any of them. Various emendations have been proposed, but are scarcely worth discussing. Many Christian interpreters since Origen have tried to read here an affirmation of immortality or resurrection, but without success: Chrysostom quite correctly refuted this interpretation with the citation of xiv 12 ff."[9] Even a note in the NABRE reads:

> The meaning of this passage is obscure because the original text
> has been poorly preserved and the ancient versions do not agree

[9] M. Pope, *Job*, AB 15 (Garden City, NY: Doubleday, 1965), 135.

among themselves. Job asserts three times that he shall see a future vindicator (Hebrew *goel*), but he leaves the time and manner of this vindication undefined. The Vulgate translation has Job indicating a belief in resurrection after death, but the Hebrew and the other ancient versions are less specific.[10]

Indeed Job 14:10-12 was cited above as an example of an Old Testament author showing no hope of an afterlife.

> But when a man dies, all vigor leaves him;
> when a mortal expires, where then is he?
> As when the waters of a lake fail,
> or a stream shrivels and dries up,
> So mortals lie down, never to rise.
> Until the heavens are no more, they shall not awake,
> nor be roused out of their sleep. (NABRE)

The same chapter goes on to claim that were one to live again, the situation might be different (v. 14) but as water wears away the stone and floods wash away soil, God destroys the hope of mortals (v. 19). This certainly does not sound like one who hopes in an afterlife. Finally, Job 19:26 is never cited in the New Testament. The verse does not seem to have been understood as a resurrection text until much later in the Christian era.

The book of Daniel does envisage a resurrection, but only for "many." Daniel 12:2-3 claims:

> Many of those who sleep in the dust of the earth shall awake,
> some to everlasting life, and some to shame and everlasting
> contempt. Those who are wise shall shine like the brightness
> of the sky, and those who lead many to righteousness, like the
> stars forever and ever.

This chapter of Daniel, with its focus on resurrection, was written in the context of the persecution of Antiochus Epiphanes (r. 175–164 BCE). This Greek ruler meant to unify his kingdom by religion and, therefore, forbade Jewish practices that were antithetical to those efforts. Many Jews preferred death over violating their laws and customs, as is recounted in the Maccabean literature. These Jews who died for a just, godly cause would surely be rewarded. Perhaps J. J. Collins sums it up best by saying "there is virtually unanimous

---

[10] See note in NABRE for Job 19:25-27.

Daniel—only generally accepted reference to resurrection

agreement among modern scholars that Daniel is referring to the actual resurrection of individuals from the dead, because of the explicit language of everlasting life. This is, in fact, the only generally accepted reference to resurrection in the Hebrew Bible."[11]

We now turn our attention to the Greek Old Testament, where the deuterocanonical 2 Maccabees speaks of a resurrection to life. Unlike much of the Old Testament, 2 Maccabees was composed in Greek during the latter half of the first century BCE, as a condensed version of a larger five-volume work (2 Macc 2:23). The literature extols obedience to God's law even in the face of extreme suffering, torture, and eventual death. Those who are righteous in the face of such persecution may expect to live again, regaining their very bodies. Those who perpetrate the suffering can expect to be judged by the almighty, all-seeing God. The story of the mother whose seven sons all defy Antiochus's commands to break God's law is recounted in chapter 7 of 2 Maccabees. In this chapter the righteous go to their martyrdom claiming that because they are dying for God's laws, he will raise them to everlasting life (2 Macc 2:9).

summary: although there is some evidence for Resurrection it's scant

In concluding our brief survey of Old Testament texts, we see that although there is evidence for resurrection, it is scant. In more cases we find a belief or hope that the just will live with God; that is to say, those who died faithful to God will be rewarded by being raised up to be with him forever. Their death is not their end. The Old Testament does not speak of a resurrection of the body (recall Hebrew does not have a word for "body"). Resurrection as a Semitic concept means a return to life or a raising up of the whole person, not merely a part. Resurrection is the reversal of the state of death. Resurrection is for the just, whereas the wicked face God's judgment and punishment. Thus the stage was set for the New Testament.

We shall see that the New Testament language about resurrection echoes the world from which the image comes. One is raised by God from death to life (cf. Rom 4:25). Thus "God raised Jesus from the dead" means, in the Jewish anthropology of New Testament times, that "God returned the person Jesus to life" rather than "God raised Jesus' body from the dead while his soul continued to live eternally." So one may not be surprised to recognize that "resurrection of the body" and "resurrection of the flesh" are each terms foreign to the

---

[11] J. J. Collins, *Daniel*, Hermeneia (Minneapolis, MN: Fortress, 1993), 391–92.

New Testament. Instead, resurrection from the dead is the term most often used to convey the belief that God raised up this man Jesus whom you killed (cf. Acts 2:23-24).

Attestations to the Risen Christ

There were no witnesses to the resurrection of Jesus (though the apocryphal Gospel of Peter does describe the resurrection from an eyewitness point of view). Instead, we have primarily five different categories of attestations to the risen Christ. First, there are formulae stemming from a period earlier than Paul's writings that refer simply to Jesus' being raised (1 Cor 15:3-7; Rom 1:3-4; 4:25; Mark 8:31; Acts 2:23-24; 4:10; 5:30-31; 10:39-40). These straightforward statements, similar to a sound bite or bumper sticker, are sometimes called kerygmatic (from the Greek term *kerygma*, meaning "announcement" or "preaching"). We might imagine early Christian preachers having recourse to these quick sound bites in their preaching. Kerygmatic statements do not mention the body being raised but Jesus being raised. In fact, the word "body" does not appear in these formulae. Second, there are formulae about Jesus appearing that are also kerygmatic and make no explicit mention of a body (1 Cor 15:5-8; Luke 24:34). Third there are stories about finding the tomb empty. These stories are different from either kind of kerygmatic statement above in that the stories claim either implicitly or explicitly that the corpse is no longer in the tomb. Something happened to it. Fourth, there is a personal eyewitness claim of a New Testament author to have witnessed the risen Christ. This fourth category of attestation to the risen Christ is privileged. In all likelihood, the only New Testament author who wrote a firsthand account of his personal experience of the risen Christ was Paul. Fifth, there are appearance narratives — that is, stories about the risen Christ speaking, walking, and even eating. Unlike the passion narratives, there is no chronological order to the appearance narratives. That is to say, it is not possible to assemble all of the appearance narratives and arrange them chronologically. There are far too many differences and even blatant contradictions regarding geography, time, and other factors for all of the appearance narratives to fit neatly into one timeline. The appearance narratives are post-Pauline, but likely preserve some pre-Pauline material. We will examine these last two categories (eyewitness testimony from a New Testament author and appearance narratives) below.

Category		Scripture Citations	
1	Jesus being raised	1 Cor 15:3-7; Rom 1:3-4; 4:25; Mark 8:31; Acts 2:23-24; 4:10; 5:30-31; 10:39-40	Straightforward, kerygmatic statements
2	Jesus appearing	1 Cor 15:5-8; Luke 24:34	Straightforward, kerygmatic statements
3	Finding the tomb empty	Matt 28:1-8; Mark 16:1-8; Luke 24:1-12, 24; John 20:1-13	Narrative stating the corpse is not in the tomb
4	Personal eyewitness testimony from a New Testament author	Gal 1:16; 1 Cor 9:1; 15:8	Statement, little to no elaboration
5	Appearance narratives		Narratives, no chronological order
	A. Mary Magdalene/Women	Matt 28:9-10; Mark 16:9-11; John 20:14-18	
	B. Two Disciples	Mark 16:12-13; Luke 24:13-35	
	C.1. Assembled Disciples (Jerusalem)	Mark 16:14; Luke 24:36-43; John 20:19-20; 26-29	
	C.2.a Eleven Disciples (Galilee)	Matt 28:16-18	
	C.2.b Seven Disciples (Sea of Tiberias)	John 21:1-23	
	D. Commissioning of Disciples	Matt 28:19-20; Mark 16:15-18; Luke 24:44-49; John 20:21-23; Acts 1:6-8	
	E. Ascension	Mark 16:19-20; Luke 24:50-53; Acts 1:9-12	

Paul

Although the writings of Paul are the earliest documents we have of the New Testament, when we read Paul's letters we often assume knowledge from the gospels, which were all written later. But what would Paul's letters sound like if they were read without our knowledge of the gospels? Such an exercise can be difficult but useful, for it allows the reader to hear Paul's voice unencumbered by other New Testament voices.

Paul, for example, never describes his experience of the risen Christ. Instead, he makes reference to it only three times: "God . . . was pleased to reveal his Son to me" (Gal 1:15-16), "have I not seen Jesus our Lord" (1 Cor 9:1); and "last of all, as to one untimely born, he appeared also to me" (1 Cor 15:8).[12] None of these examples comes close to Luke's three-fold description of Paul's encounter with the risen Lord on the road to Damascus that we read in Acts 9:1-20; 22:1-16; and 26:1-20.[13] In fact, the reader of Paul's letters is left grasping for details of the encounter that Luke depicts so vividly, even if inconsistently. Paul is content to make reference to his encounter by means of these laconic statements. Throughout Christian history most theologians have read these passages in light of the gospel resurrection narratives and in light of the story Luke tells in Acts. In so doing, these theologians read Paul as though he witnessed a tangible, fleshly Christ. But today, by focusing squarely on Paul's letters and not allowing the gospel accounts to color their interpretation, more scholars find that these statements can also be read as indicating that

---

[12] This last statement comes at the conclusion of a list to which Paul appends himself.

> he appeared to Cephas, then to the Twelve. After that, he appeared to more than five hundred brothers at once, most of whom are still living, though some have fallen asleep. After that he appeared to James, then to all the apostles. Last of all, as to one born abnormally, he appeared to me (1 Cor 15:5-8; NABRE).

These are not stories of appearances but claims of appearances that buttress the kerygma "he was raised" (1 Cor 15:4a). As the burial confirms the death (1 Cor 15:3-4a) so the appearances confirm that he was raised (1 Cor 15:4b-8). Of all the people to whom Christ appeared, we have only Paul's writings.

[13] See appendix A, table 2.

Paul had an interior, subjective, though no less real experience of the Risen Lord.[14]

Gospels

A majority of Paul's letters were written in the 50s CE. The earliest canonical gospel (Mark) was written in the late 60s. Matthew and Luke were written independently of one another in the 80s and the Gospel of John did not find its final form until around the 90s. It is a widely held opinion among scholars that none of the four evangelists were eyewitnesses to Jesus' earthly ministry. Instead, the evangelists most likely used sources in composing their gospels, as Luke himself candidly admits (Luke 1:1-4).

The church recognizes that there was a three-stage formation of the gospels (DV 19).[15] The first stage is the teaching and actions performed by Jesus of Nazareth in roughly the first third of the first century CE. The second stage is postresurrectional, consisting of followers preaching about Jesus' sayings and actions. This second stage includes apostolic preaching, kerygmatic statements, catechetical formulas, liturgy and/or worship, hymns and songs, and storytelling — roughly corresponding to the middle third of the first century CE. The third stage of gospel formation is when the evangelists culled material from the second stage and shaped it in light of their audience. The third stage occurred in the last third of the first century CE. One sees, according to this brief schema, that the evangelists did not compose their gospels during the earthly life of Jesus but instead relied on the testimony of others about the apostolic preaching and teaching about Jesus.

Mark

We turn our attention first to the earliest of the four gospels, Mark, for whom the appearance stories did not seem to be part of the tradition. Three times in the Gospel of Mark Jesus predicts his passion, death, and resurrection. Yet there is no prediction of an appearance

---

[14] B. Schmisek, "Paul's Vision of the Risen Lord," *BTB* (2011).

[15] See also *On the Historicity of the Gospels*, Pontifical Biblical Commission (1964).

(8:31; 9:31; 10:33-34).[16] The resurrection account in Mark is complicated by the fact that there are multiple endings to the gospel.[17] Even
the notes in the NABRE inform the modern reader of a shorter ending,
a longer ending, and the Freer logion. Other endings to the gospel
also exist. The best Greek manuscripts of the gospel end with 16:1-8.

> When the sabbath was over, Mary Magdalene, Mary, the mother
> of James, and Salome bought spices so that they might go and
> anoint him. Very early when the sun had risen, on the first day
> of the week, they came to the tomb. They were saying to one
> another, "Who will roll back the stone for us from the entrance
> to the tomb?" When they looked up, they saw that the stone had
> been rolled back; it was very large. On entering the tomb they
> saw a young man sitting on the right side, clothed in a white
> robe, and they were utterly amazed. He said to them, "Do not
> be amazed! You seek Jesus of Nazareth, the crucified. He has
> been raised; he is not here. Behold the place where they laid
> him. But go and tell his disciples and Peter, 'He is going before
> you to Galilee; there you will see him, as he told you.'" Then
> they went out and fled from the tomb, seized with trembling
> and bewilderment. They said nothing to anyone, for they were
> afraid. (Mark 16:1-8; NABRE)

The story is that of finding the empty tomb. This is not an appearance narrative, though an appearance is certainly promised (16:7).
The stone has already been rolled away by the time the women arrive. The women are greeted not by an angel but by a young man
(*neaniskon*) who was already sitting down in the tomb. Afraid, the
women ran away.

To one who is already a believer, these issues might not seem too
critical. But to those who do not believe, the holes in the story are gap-

---

[16] It should be noted that both Matthew and Luke follow Mark in lacking
the prediction of an appearance, even though each gospel has resurrection
appearance narratives.

[17] The longer ending (16:9-20) to the Gospel of Mark can be outlined this
way:

1. 16:9-11 Appearance to Mary Magdalene
2. 16:12-13 Appearance to Two Disciples
3. 16:14-18 Commissioning of the Eleven
4. 16:19-20 Ascension of Jesus

ing. Who rolled away the stone? When was the stone rolled away? Who is the man? Where did he come from? Might he have stolen the body? Why did the women run away afraid, not saying anything to anyone and not believing he had been raised from the dead after three days, as he had foretold (Mark 8:31; 9:31; 10:34)? With an ending like Mark 16:1-8, one may want another ending. So perhaps we are not too surprised to read, alongside the shorter ending, a longer ending, the Freer logion, and other endings. It has been demonstrated that these endings (especially the longer ending) are dependent on stories in the other canonical gospels.[18] For our purposes, let us note that the earliest gospel has no appearance narrative and leaves many questions unanswered.

Matthew

It seems Matthew, who used Mark as a source for his gospel, found Mark's conclusion (Mark 16:1-8) wanting. Matthew, in effect, rewrote and expanded it. Matthew's resurrection account has grown to 20 verses, outlined here:

1. 28:1-8   Discovery of the Empty Tomb (based on Mark)
2. 28:9-10   Appearance to the women
3. 28:11-15 The origin of the false story
4. 28:16-20 Appearance to the eleven disciples /
             Great Commission

Matthew does follow Mark in the first eight verses, but even here he has developed the story.

> After the sabbath, as the first day of the week was dawning, Mary Magdalene and the other Mary came to see the tomb. And behold, there was a great earthquake; for an angel of the Lord descended from heaven, approached, rolled back the stone, and sat upon it. His appearance was like lightning and his clothing was white as snow. The guards were shaken with fear of him and became like dead men. Then the angel said to the women in reply, "Do not be afraid! I know that you are seeking Jesus the crucified. He is

[18] See, for example, James A. Kelhoffer, *Miracle and Mission: The Authentication of Missionaries and Their Message in the Longer Ending of Mark* (Tübingen: Mohr-Siebeck, 2000).

not here, for he has been raised just as he said. Come and see the place where he lay. Then go quickly and tell his disciples, 'He has been raised from the dead, and he is going before you to Galilee; there you will see him.' Behold, I have told you." Then they went away quickly from the tomb, fearful yet overjoyed, and ran to announce this to his disciples. (Matt 28:1-8; NABRE)

Matthew has added apocalyptic elements (earthquake, angel descending from heaven, etc.) and eliminated the women wondering who will roll the stone away (Mark 16:3-4). Matthew can eliminate the wonder because in his story the angel of the Lord rolled back the stone. The women depart not only fearful as they did in Mark but also "overjoyed." The women do in fact announce the good news to the disciples. These changes (scholars call them "redactions") in the story "clean up" many of the problems that exist in Mark's resurrection account.

Yet, simply redacting Mark's eight-verse conclusion is not enough for Matthew, who also composes 28:9-20. Though there may be pre-Matthean material (appearance to the women, Jesus' appearance in Galilee, the claim that the disciples stole the body of Jesus), the material has been so thoroughly reworked by Matthew that it is impossible to recover with certainty historically reliable details.

And behold, Jesus met them on their way and greeted them. They approached, embraced his feet, and did him homage. Then Jesus said to them, "Do not be afraid. Go tell my brothers to go to Galilee, and there they will see me." While they were going, some of the guard went into the city and told the chief priests all that had happened. They assembled with the elders and took counsel; then they gave a large sum of money to the soldiers, telling them, "You are to say, 'His disciples came by night and stole him while we were asleep.' And if this gets to the ears of the governor, we will satisfy [him] and keep you out of trouble." The soldiers took the money and did as they were instructed. And this story has circulated among the Jews to the present [day].

The eleven disciples went to Galilee, to the mountain to which Jesus had ordered them. When they saw him, they worshiped, but they doubted. Then Jesus approached and said to them, "All power in heaven and on earth has been given to me. Go, therefore, and make disciples of all nations, baptizing them in the name of the Father, and of the Son, and of the holy Spirit, teaching them to observe all that I have commanded you. And behold, I am with you always, until the end of the age." (Matt 28:9-20; NABRE)

In Matthew, unlike the story in Mark 16:1-8, the reader knows that Jesus himself appeared to the women and spoke to them. That the women clung to his feet is Matthew's way of showing the tangibility of the resurrected Christ. This is Matthew's way of saying, like Luke, that the risen Christ was no ghost. The story of the appearance to the women has echoes in John 20:14-18: Mary Magdalene's presence, the appearance happens before Jesus appeared to the disciples, the appearance takes place near the tomb, the woman touches/clings to Jesus (an action that Jesus stops), and Jesus commands the woman to tell the disciples (brothers) to go to Galilee where they will see him.[19]

In the next section (Matt 28:11-15) the reader discovers the origin of the claim that the disciples stole the body of Jesus. In the final section of the chapter (Matt 28:16-20), the disciples themselves see the risen Jesus (yet some doubt) and receive what later scholars refer to as the "Great Commission," to go out teaching and baptizing. In this story tangibility is not the issue. Jesus promises to be with them until the end of the age. Perhaps curiously to the modern reader, there is no ascension. We rely on Luke for that story.

Matthew has thus clarified the story he inherited from Mark and even made it "better" by introducing apocalyptic elements, an apologia for the claim that the disciples stole Jesus' body, the Easter proclamation to the disciples, and appearances of the risen Jesus to the women and to the disciples themselves. In introducing the first appearance story, Matthew has also introduced the tangibility of the resurrected Jesus. Even so, tangibility is not mentioned in the second story (28:16-20). By answering questions that Mark's gospel left open, Matthew introduced new questions: what happened to Jesus after the resurrection appearances? Did the disciples doubt because they experienced only a vision or ghost of Jesus?

---

[19] C. H. Dodd, "The Appearance of the Risen Christ: An Essay in Form Criticism of the Gospels" in *Studies in the Gospels*, ed. D. E. Nineham (Oxford: Oxford University Press, 1955): 33, argues that the story in Mark 16:9-11 preserves a story independent of the canonical gospels. I agree with A. Y. Collins, *Mark*, Hermeneia (Minneapolis, MN: Fortress, 2007), 807–8, that Mark 16:9-11 is probably dependent on John 20:14-18 and Matthew 28:9-10.

Luke

Matthew is not the only evangelist to have had Mark's resurrection account at hand when writing. A majority of scholars maintain that Luke and Matthew wrote independently, though each used Mark as a source. Luke, the evangelist who candidly reveals he was not an eyewitness (Luke 1:1-4), gives us the most graphic description of a fleshly, risen Christ. And as we saw in chapter 1, Ignatius of Antioch seems to have followed Luke in claiming that Christ rose in the flesh. Luke's resurrected Christ is a source for those scenes of Jesus portrayed in the final moments of the Franco Zeffirelli film *Jesus of Nazareth* or more recently the Mel Gibson film *Passion of the Christ*. In those films, the resurrected Jesus appears akin to the earthly Jesus. It is as though the earthly Jesus had been in hibernation and returns to the living. The cinematic portrayal of the resurrected Jesus as a flesh and blood human being has its roots in Luke's narrative.

We would do well to remember that Luke has a tendency to objectivize the supernatural—that is, he can make it into an object. For example, if we examine the stories of the baptism of Jesus, Mark is followed by Matthew in saying that the spirit descended on Jesus "like a dove" (Mark 1:10; Matt 3:16). Only Luke says that the spirit descended "in bodily form like a dove" (Luke 3:22). Luke is a master storyteller. His accounts provide rich material for artists. One downside, however, is that by objectivizing the supernatural one might underestimate the reality of the mystery. The baptism of Jesus is more than the appearance of a dove.

At fifty-three verses, Luke has the longest resurrection chapter of any gospel. Many (including the notes of the NABRE) have indicated that the chapter can be divided into five parts:

1. 24:1-12   The women at the empty tomb[20]
2. 24:13-35   The appearance to the two disciples on the way to Emmaus
3. 24:36-43   The appearance to the disciples in Jerusalem

---

[20] The notes from the NABRE begin this section at 23:56b rather than 24:1. That half verse reads, "then they rested on the sabbath according to the commandment" (NABRE). However, 24:1 is preferred as the start of the section as it corresponds to Mark 16:1. Luke 23:56b more properly belongs to the conclusion of Luke 23.

4. 24:44-49   Jesus' final instructions
5. 24:50-53   The ascension

Most of the first section (Luke 24:1-12) corresponds generally to Mark 16:1-8. A complicating feature of the Lukan account is verse 12, which is in the oldest Greek manuscripts but not in all later manuscripts. It is italicized below.

> But at daybreak on the first day of the week they took the spices they had prepared and went to the tomb. They found the stone rolled away from the tomb; but when they entered, they did not find the body of the Lord Jesus. While they were puzzling over this, behold, two men in dazzling garments appeared to them. They were terrified and bowed their faces to the ground. They said to them, "Why do you seek the living one among the dead? He is not here, but he has been raised. Remember what he said to you while he was still in Galilee, that the Son of Man must be handed over to sinners and be crucified, and rise on the third day." And they remembered his words. Then they returned from the tomb and announced all these things to the eleven and to all the others. The women were Mary Magdalene, Joanna, and Mary the mother of James; the others who accompanied them also told this to the apostles, but their story seemed like nonsense and they did not believe them. *But Peter got up and ran to the tomb, bent down, and saw the burial cloths alone; then he went home amazed at what had happened.* (Luke 24:1-12; NABRE)

Luke, like Matthew, has "improved" the story he received by addressing some of the issues unclear in Mark. For example, the women arrive at the tomb to find the stone rolled away, as in Mark. Yet, Luke speaks of *two* men (*andres*) in *dazzling garments* (not merely Mark's lone "young man"). The dazzling garments are apparently meant to indicate that the two are angels, for that is how Luke refers to them later in the story (24:23). The two cite the words of Jesus by which he said he would rise. The women then recall those words and (apparently) believe, unlike the disciples who dismiss the story as nonsense and do not believe. Like Matthew, Luke also adds material not found in Mark and extends the story first by saying that Peter in fact ran to the tomb, found it empty, and was amazed.

Verse 12 may preserve an ancient tradition of an appearance to Peter (cf. 1 Cor 15:5). Raymond Brown considers the verse an interpolation by a redactor[21] whereas Fitzmyer insists that the verse "has to be regarded as part of the original text of the Lucan Gospel."[22] The verse of course tells a story not of an appearance to Peter, but of Peter finding the empty tomb. Even at that, Peter is not said to "believe"; rather, he is "amazed." Later, the reader will learn that the Lord did eventually appear to Simon (24:35).

The story of the Road to Emmaus (Luke 24:13-35) might, on first glance, provide more evidence for the nature of the Risen Christ. Mark 16:12-13, part of the "longer ending," may preserve an earlier and certainly much shorter version of the story. But as the Lukan story goes, on Easter Sunday, Jesus walked along the road to Emmaus with Cleopas and another disciple, both of whom did not recognize him. The three become engaged in a discussion about Scripture and its fulfillment in light of the recent events. Only when Jesus "breaks the bread" do the two disciples come to know him, at which point Jesus vanishes, presumably returning to glory. The disciples return to Jerusalem only to discover that the eleven and their companions were saying that the Lord had appeared to Simon.

Various scholars interpret this Emmaus story in various ways. It should be noted that though the story may preserve pre-Lukan elements (the name Cleopas, for example, may be either pre-Lukan or a Lukan creation) this pericope is laden with Lukan theological and geographical themes including being on the road, fulfilling prophecy, vanishing upon recognition, and Eucharist.[23] Though the appearance includes an apparently tangible risen Christ walking, speaking, reclining, taking bread (though not necessarily eating it), and more, it has certainly been dramatized by Luke to the degree that it is nearly impossible to recover any historically reliable details. In this way the story may be like the story of Paul's calling in Acts. It too has been dramatized by Luke such that it is nearly impossible to recover historically reliable details.

In the next three sections (the appearance to the disciples in Jerusalem [Luke 24:36-43]; Jesus' final instructions [Luke 24:44-49]; and the ascension [Luke 24:50-53]), all taking place on Easter Sunday, Luke

---

[21] R. E. Brown, *The Gospel According to John: XIII–XXI*, AB 29A (New York: Doubleday, 1970), 1000.

[22] J. A. Fitzmyer, *The Gospel According to Luke: X–XXIV*, AB 28A (New York: Doubleday, 1985), 1542.

[23] Ibid., 1557–59.

relates stories of many people encountering the risen Jesus, who is found to be "flesh and bones" and "not a ghost." Though Matthew has the women clinging to the feet of the risen Jesus, in Luke the risen Jesus even eats a meal with the disciples. In his second book, Luke emphasizes that the body of Jesus did not experience decay (Acts 2:27; 13:35, 37). Luke concludes his gospel by describing graphically the ascension and thereby answering the question: where is Jesus now? Jesus is in heaven. Thus the evangelist who admits he was not an eyewitness gives the reader the most physically graphic depiction of the risen Christ.

Luke sets the tone that the Gospel of John and the Johannine redactor echo for the graphic physical portrayal of the resurrection of Jesus. When the resurrection is portrayed in such physical terms, one may fall into the danger of understanding resurrection as resuscitation. Of course, the resurrection of Jesus transcends even the category of resurrection. Though the early Christians spoke of Jesus' resurrection, it is clear that Luke meant more by it than the resurrection of Jairus' daughter (Luke 8:54-55), or the raised son of the widow of Nain (Luke 7:15). In each of the gospels, Jesus' own resurrection was something qualitatively different. Lazarus (John 11:43-44; 12:1-2), Jairus's daughter, and the son of the widow of Nain all died at a later time. Jesus, once raised from the dead, is no longer subject to death. Still, the physically graphic portrayal of the resurrected Jesus may leave room for misunderstanding.

John

The Gospel of John has two entire chapters devoted to the resurrected Jesus. Together these two chapters comprise some of the most difficult material having to do with the resurrection. It is common scholarly opinion that these difficulties arise because each chapter is from a different author and each chapter has evidence of later redactional efforts. As a result, though John has the most material, much of it is late, of questionable historical veracity, and laden with theological *gravitas*.

John 20 has a series of resurrection stories that may or may not have been related before the composition of this chapter. That is to say, the author of John 20 may have been privy to disparate source material that he combined in writing this chapter. Or, disparate elements of source material had been combined before the author had access to it. There are two main sections of chapter 20: events at the tomb (20:1-18) and events at the house (20:19-29), followed by the conclusion to the gospel (20:30-31).

An outline of chapter 20:

1. 20:1-18   Events at the tomb
   a. 20:1-2   Mary Magdala finding the tomb empty: part one
   b. 20:3-10   Peter and the Beloved Disciple finding the tomb empty
   c. 20:11-13   Mary Magdala finding the tomb empty: part two
   d. 20:14-18   Risen Christ appears to Mary

2. 20:19-29   Events at the tomb
   a. 20:19-23   Jesus appears to assembled disciples
   b. 20:24-25   Transitional/explanatory note
   c. 20:26-29   Jesus appears to assembled disciples including Thomas

3. 20:30-31   Conclusion

In the first main section (20:1-18), Mary of Magdala comes to the tomb to find the stone had been rolled away. She immediately leaves the scene to tell Peter and the disciple whom Jesus loved. Together they discover the empty tomb. The disciple whom Jesus loved is the first to believe. He and Peter return while Mary stays behind at the tomb where she sees "two angels." After a brief conversation with them she turns around to see Jesus, though she does not recognize him immediately. Only when Jesus addresses her by name does she realize who he is with the acclamation "Rabbouni" or "my master." Mary is then commanded to tell the disciples, which she does with the Easter proclamation "I have seen the Lord."

Here we follow Brown's lead in detecting traces of three narratives that were combined at some point (whether by the author or before is impossible to say). There are two narratives of visits to the empty tomb and one narrative of an appearance of Jesus to Mary Magdalene.[24] The first narrative of a visit to the empty tomb corre-

---

[24] Brown, *John*, 998.

sponds roughly to the narratives in other gospels about the women finding the tomb empty (John 20:1-2; 11-13; cf. Mark 16:1-8; Matt 28:1-8; Luke 24:1-11). The second narrative of Peter and/or others finding the tomb empty has traces in Luke 24:12, 24. The story of the risen Christ appearing to Mary (John 20:14-18) corresponds roughly to Matthew 28:9-10 (as we saw earlier). Matthew 28:9-10 and John 20:14-18 together are the likely source for Mark 16:9-11. Many scholars will accept the hypothesis that there was one ancient tradition of an appearance to Mary Magdalene behind the appearance narratives as we have them. Thus, Matthew and John would have each shaped and developed the tradition to serve their own theological interests.[25] Even so, Mary Magdalene, unlike Paul, is not a New Testament author. Granted that Mary Magdalene witnessed the risen Christ, we do not have the story in her own words but in the words of later evangelists, tailored to their own theological ends.

In the second main section (20:19-29), we essentially have the expansion of one resurrection narrative of the appearance of Jesus to the assembled disciples. This narrative has similarities with Luke and Mark 16:14 (which place the event in Jerusalem), and also with Matthew and John 21 (which place the event in Galilee), though the place of the resurrection appearance is not pertinent to our immediate scope. The expansion in John 20 seems to have been composed to address certain theological issues that we will discuss briefly.

> On the evening of that first day of the week, when the doors were locked, where the disciples were, for fear of the Jews, Jesus came and stood in their midst and said to them, "Peace be with you." When he had said this, he showed them his hands and his side. The disciples rejoiced when they saw the Lord. [Jesus] said to them again, "Peace be with you. As the Father has sent me, so I send you." And when he had said this, he breathed on them and said to them, "Receive the holy Spirit. Whose sins you forgive are forgiven them, and whose sins you retain are retained."
>
> Thomas, called Didymus, one of the Twelve, was not with them when Jesus came. So the other disciples said to him, "We have seen the Lord." But he said to them, "Unless I see the mark of the nails in his hands and put my finger into the nailmarks and put my hand into his side, I will not believe." Now a week later

---

[25] Ibid., 1003–4.

his disciples were again inside and Thomas was with them. Jesus
came, although the doors were locked, and stood in their midst
and said, "Peace be with you." Then he said to Thomas, "Put
your finger here and see my hands, and bring your hand and put
it into my side, and do not be unbelieving, but believe." Thomas
answered and said to him, "My Lord and my God!" Jesus said
to him, "Have you come to believe because you have seen me?
Blessed are those who have not seen and have believed." (John
20:19-29; NABRE)

John, like Luke's comment about flesh and blood, places emphasis on
the body of Jesus. In the first scene, John indicates that Jesus shows
the disciples his side and his hands. Yet even this may strike the
reader as odd. Why did Jesus show the disciples his side and his
hands? Brown argues that the underlying story initially conveyed the
disciples as doubting (as we find in Luke where they are startled, or in
Matthew when the disciples worship the risen Jesus but doubt). The
Gospel of John has transferred that doubt to the character of Thomas,
yet retained the notion of Jesus showing the disciples his side and his
hands. That line also serves to prefigure the Thomas story.

In the second scene, with Thomas present, Jesus invites Thomas to
probe his side and his hands so that he might not continue in disbelief
but believe. Most scholars would agree that the Thomas story was
written by the evangelist for apologetic ends. That is to say, Thomas
represents one who does not believe in the resurrection of Jesus or at
least doubts it. Jesus' words to Thomas are, in effect, words to anyone
who would doubt: "Blessed are those who have not seen and have
believed." Though the story never says Thomas probed the side and
hands of Jesus, he still proclaims Jesus as "My Lord and My God,"
which is a christological claim par excellence and uniquely Johannine.

Thus, the graphic display of the risen Jesus in the second scene can
be understood as a later redactional element to address theological
issues surrounding belief in the risen Jesus. Apparently, a physically
present, with wounds visible, risen Jesus was more reliable than a
claim such as "I have seen the Lord."

The epilogue of the Gospel of John (chapter 21) has further challenges. Why, after a clear conclusion to the gospel (20:30-31), is there
yet another story of a resurrection appearance, another chapter to the
gospel? Why did the disciples return to fishing after having witnessed
the risen Christ? Why did the disciples not recognize the risen Christ

after having seen him twice? In light of these and many such questions, we are not surprised to learn that a vast majority of scholars hold that this chapter was written by a later redactor. The chapter was added to address many issues pertinent to the Johannine community vis-à-vis the larger Christian community, as well as the (unexpected) death of the beloved disciple himself.

A brief outline of the chapter will serve to highlight the two main stories therein:

1. 21:1-14   Appearance to the disciples at the Sea of Tiberias
   a. 21:1-8   Fishing
   b. 21:9-13   Meal
   c. 21:14   Editor's note

2. 21:15-23   Jesus speaks to Peter
   a. 21:15-17   Rehabilitation of Peter
   b. 21:18-23   Fate of Peter and the Fate of the Beloved Disciple

3. 21:24-25   Another conclusion

The most important pericope for our purposes in John 21 is the appearance by the seashore. In this story, Jesus is portrayed as preparing a meal, much like the appearance story in Luke. The physicality of the resurrection is emphasized. However, unlike Luke, John does not portray Jesus eating the meal. In fact, though this is the third time the disciples had witnessed the risen Christ they still did not know that it was Jesus (21:4). The beloved disciple however is the first to recognize him. Even after Jesus invites them to eat not one dares to inquire "who are you" "for they knew it was the Lord." Yet, why does the author add that comment? Why would the disciples have had to ask "Who are you?" And why is it significant that they did not ask "Who are you?" Some scholars find clues in these statements that this story reflects at least one version of the first appearance to Peter by the risen Christ.[26] This resurrection narrative does not so much "prove" the corporeality of the risen Jesus as much as it is a likely narrative dramatization of the appearance written to address

[26] E.g., Brown, *John*, 1085–87.

then-current theological problems such as the relationship between the beloved disciple and Peter, a theme that would be developed in the next episode (vv 15-23). The other stories in the epilogue add little to our understanding of the resurrected Christ when we see that they are most likely etiological (i.e., written to explain then-current theological or other problems).

Thus, after examining the gospel writers' accounts of the resurrection of Jesus we come to some interesting conclusions. The earliest account (Mark) has no resurrection appearance at all; rather, there is the finding of the empty tomb. Only the later gospels include an appearance narrative. Each of the later accounts develops earlier material or is a composition of the evangelists. Many of the accounts include elements whereby the individuals do not recognize Jesus (Mark 16:12; Luke 24:16, 37; John 20:14; 21:4). Yet this lack of recognition is combined with an emphasis on the physical or bodily resurrection. Indeed, the apologetic character of the later resurrection narratives could indicate that the evangelists were trying to counteract the idea that the risen Jesus was akin to a ghost. Matthew tells a story of the women touching the feet of Jesus. Luke's risen Jesus walks, shares a meal, and states flatly that he has flesh and bones. John's risen Jesus and that of the epilogue attest to physicality as well. The later narratives are simply more graphic than the earlier.

There is little, if any, ancient material that is preserved in the resurrection narratives to indicate that the resurrected Jesus was tangible. Instead, the graphic elements in the stories are developments from later periods, or compositions of the evangelists. The stories may have been added in part to address questions about corporeality. The tangibility of the risen Christ in the stories "proves" the resurrection in a way that a revelation (Gal 1:16), an appearance (1 Cor 9:1; 15:8), or the empty tomb (Mark 16:1-8) might not.

We recall that the one eyewitness to the risen Christ who has given us a written record of the encounter, Paul, does not describe the event. The Easter proclamation of Paul, Mary Magdalene and others is "I have seen the Lord." It is not "I have seen the body of Jesus." Early Christians encountered the living Christ. One way they expressed this encounter was to say that Jesus himself, not merely a part of him, had been raised from the dead. God had reversed the death of Jesus and raised him to life. The early Christians used this image because it was part of the religious milieu (cf. Dan 12:2-3; 2 Macc 7).

Even if the Sadducees categorically rejected it (Acts 23:8), Jews of the first century, including the disciples of Jesus, were familiar with the image of resurrection. When these disciples encountered Jesus after his death, they interpreted that experience with the category or metaphor of resurrection.

That category was appropriate because it expressed the belief that God has raised Jesus from the dead — that is to say, the early Christians believed that the person of Jesus, the totality of Jesus, everything it means to be Jesus, was not dead but alive. What human beings did by killing Jesus had been overcome by God's raising Jesus. One weakness with this metaphor is that it very quickly moves to a fleshly understanding of the living Jesus. The risen Jesus is seen to be composed of "flesh and bones." This physical understanding would then give rise to new questions such as, where is the risen body of Jesus now? The resurrection image conjures up the idea of Lazarus rising from the dead or Jairus' daughter being raised. But the category of resurrection falls short when applied to Jesus for he had been raised to "new life," never to die again. For the New Testament authors, the resurrection of Jesus is more than mere resuscitation. Unlike Tertullian, who as we saw earlier maintained that Lazarus was the "pre-eminent instance of resurrection,"[27] we recognize that the New Testament authors believed the resurrection of Jesus to be something qualitatively different. As such, the category of resurrection was only one of the many categories, images, and metaphors that early New Testament authors used to speak of what happened to Jesus after his death. We will explore other prominent images and metaphors below.

Other Metaphors

As a reminder, the term metaphor is "a figure of speech in which a name or descriptive word or phrase is transferred to an object or action different from but analogous to, that to which it is literally applicable; an instance of this, a metaphorical expression."[28] Though "resurrection," "raised [from the dead]," "God raised him/Jesus" or some variant thereof is the overwhelmingly predominant New

---

[27] Tertullian, *De Resurrectione*, 53.3.
[28] *OED*, s.v. "metaphor."

Testament metaphor to speak of what happened to Jesus after his death,[29] New Testament authors use many other metaphors.[30] Eleven of the twenty-seven books in the New Testament never use the term "resurrection" of Jesus if at all.[31] Yet at times, modern Christians seem to forget or at least neglect the many other metaphors used to speak of what happened to Christ after his death. As we explored the background to the term resurrection/raised from the dead, we shall offer a brief survey of some of the other prominent metaphors and some background material useful to understanding their application to Jesus after his death. Though there are many images,[32] we will focus on eight: (1) sitting/seated/standing at God's right hand,[33] (2) exalted/exaltation/being lifted up,[34] (3) glorified/ taken up in glory / enter into his glory,[35] (4) ascension (taken up / lifted up),[36] (5) going to the Father,[37] (6) vindicated in the Spirit,[38] (7) in paradise/

---

[29] Matt 16:21; 17:9, 23; 20:19; 27:53; 28:6, 7; Mark 8:31; 9:9, 31; 10:34; 14:28; 16:6, 9, 14; Luke 9:22; 18:33; 24:7, 34, 46; John 2:22; 20:9; 21:14; Acts 1:22; 2:31, 32; 3:15, 26; 4:2, 10, 33; 5:30; 10:4, 40; 13:30, 33, 34, 37; 17:3, 31; 26:23; Rom 1:4; 4:24, 25; 6:5; 7:4; 8:11, 34; 10:9; 1 Cor 6:14; 15:12, 13, 15, 21; 2 Cor 4:14; Gal 1:1; Eph 1:20; 2:6; Phil 3:10; Col 2:12; 1 Thess 1:10; 4:14; 2 Tim 2:8; Heb 6:2; 1 Pet 1:3, 21; 3:21.

[30] The terms "metaphor" and "image" are used here interchangeably.

[31] The following books do not use the term resurrection or any variant thereof: 2 Thessalonians, 1 Timothy, Titus, Philemon, James, 2 Peter, 1 John, 2 John, 3 John, and Jude. Though the book of Revelation speaks of a first and a second resurrection, it does not use the term explicitly of Jesus. However, Revelation 1:5 does refer to Jesus as "firstborn of the dead" (as does Col 1:18).

[32] Some others might be: Christ's becoming High Priest (Heb 1:4; 6:20; 7:26), becoming "perfected" (Heb 2:10; 5:9), "put to death in the flesh, he was brought to life in the spirit" (1 Pet 3:18), "Jesus Christ, who has gone into heaven" (1 Pet 3:22), and "firstborn of the dead" (Rev 1:5).

[33] Matt 22:44; 26:64; Mark 14:62; 16:19; Luke 22:69; Acts 2:33, 34; 5:31; 7:55; cf. Acts 5:31; Rom 8:34; Eph 1:20-21; Col 3:1; Heb 1:3, 13; 8:1; 10:12; 12:2; 1 Pet 3:22.

[34] John 3:14; 8:28; 12:32-34; Acts 2:33; 5:31; 2 Cor 11:7; Phil 2:9.

[35] Luke 24:26; John 7:39; 12:16, 23; 16:14; 17:4-5; Acts 3:13; Rom 8:17; Phil 3:21; Heb 2:7, 9; 1 Tim 3:16; 1 Pet 1:21; 2 Pet 1:17.

[36] Mark 16:19; Luke 24:51; John 20:17; Acts 1:2, 9, 11, 22; 1 Tim 3:16; cf. Eph 4:8.

[37] John 14:12, 28; 16:5, 10, 17, 28.

[38] 1 Tim 3:16.

heaven,[39] and (8) entering the heavenly holy of holies.[40] One must also note that the metaphors are not sharp and distinct. Instead, many of the images overlap. One image may flow into another to produce a slightly different understanding (for example: seated at God's right hand, exalted to God's right hand, exalted, exalted to glory, lifted up to glory, taken up into glory, or lifted up). Although sharp distinctions cannot be made, categorization may serve as a useful organizational framework (see appendix D).

We will discuss the background to the image and why it might have been applied to Jesus (how the term/metaphor expressed some fundamental belief about what happened to Jesus after his death). We will conclude each section with some positive aspects of the image/metaphor and also some potential negatives when the metaphor or image is pressed too far.

Seated at God's Right Hand

The idea of being at God's right hand or being seated at his right hand comes primarily from royal enthronement psalms such as 110:1, but also Isaiah 63:10 and *Ps. Sol.* 13:1. Scholars believe that Psalm 110 was sung when a new Davidic king took the throne. We might imagine a troubadour or court singer intoning for the king the psalm (in its entirety here) as part of a coronation ceremony:

> The LORD says to my lord: "Sit at my right hand,
> while I make your enemies your footstool."
> The scepter of your might:
> the LORD extends your strong scepter from Zion.
> Have dominion over your enemies!
> Yours is princely power from the day of your birth.
> In holy splendor before the daystar,
> like dew I begot you.
> The LORD has sworn and will not waver:
> "You are a priest forever in the manner of Melchizedek."
> At your right hand is the Lord,
> who crushes kings on the day of his wrath,
> Who judges nations, heaps up corpses,

---

[39] Luke 23:43.
[40] Heb 9:1-28, esp. 9:12, 24-26.

> crushes heads across the wide earth,
> Who drinks from the brook by the wayside
> and thus holds high his head. (Ps 110:1-7; NABRE)

The court singer introduces his song to the king as his lord. Then, speaking on behalf of the LORD (i.e., God), assures the king that the LORD will vanquish the king's enemies. The king is the LORD's begotten, a priest forever, who will be accompanied by the LORD in future battles.

The Old Testament image of sitting at the right of God conveys royal power and enthronement. In antiquity, one who sat at the king's right hand enjoyed the favor, status, and power of the king.[41] Thus upon enthronement, the king of Judah himself was said to be seated at the right hand of God, and thereby to enjoy the favor, status, and power of God.

Many New Testament authors use this metaphor, sometimes quoting or alluding to Psalm 110:1, to reflect the belief that Jesus, after his death, now enjoys the favor, status, and power of God.[42] In the Synoptic Gospels, Jesus replies to those who query whether he is the Messiah with "I am, and you will see the Son of Man sitting on the right hand of the Power [allusion to Psalm 110:1] and coming with the clouds of heaven [allusion to Dan 7:13]" (Matt 22:44; with a parallel in Mark 14:62). The future exaltation of Jesus is cast in the imagery of Psalm 110:1. Not only will Jesus be vindicated but he will return, as the retort "you will see" coupled with the allusion to Daniel 7:13 implies.

A weakness of the "at the right hand of God" image might be that it can be taken literally to imagine a seat next to God. For example, a student once asked "If Jesus is seated at God's right hand, who is at God's left?" This kind of question has the potential of reducing the metaphor to absurdity and may strip it of its meaning, which is not that Jesus has a chair especially for him, next to God. Rather, Jesus now enjoys the favor, status, and power of God. Since we do not live

---

[41] Cf. D. M. Hay, *Glory at the Right Hand: Psalm 110 in Early Christianity*, SBLMS 18 (Nash, 1973).

[42] Matt 22:44; 26:64; Mark 14:62; 16:19; Luke 22:69; Acts 2:33, 34; 5:31; 7:55; cf. Acts 5:31; Rom 8:34; Eph 1:20-21; Col 3:1; Heb 1:3, 13; 8:1; 10:12; 12:2; 1 Pet 3:22.

in ancient times, when being seated next to the king meant that one shared the king's status, favor, and power, the image may need to be explained today. On the positive side, this image hearkens back to the psalms and the kingship, thereby demonstrating not only the Israelite roots of the metaphor but also Jesus' Davidic kingship.

Exalted / Lifted Up

Another popular New Testament metaphor to express Jesus' risen status is exaltation,[43] which is used to express something similar to "seated at God's right hand." Acts 2:33 combines both images and reads, "Having been exalted to the right hand of God" (cf. Acts 5:31). The Hebrew term *gābah*, meaning "to be high" or "to be exalted,"[44] is used in Ezekiel 21:31 and Isaiah 52:13. "Thus says the Lord GOD: Off with the turban and away with the crown! Nothing shall be as it was! Exalt the lowly and bring the exalted low!" (Ezek 21:31; NABRE). Ezekiel imagines here the upsetting of the normal order, where the priest and prince (signaled by turban and crown) are dismissed. The lowly are exalted and the exalted brought low. The canticle of Mary in the Gospel of Luke follows this pattern of reversal when it reads "He has thrown down the rulers from their thrones but lifted up [*hypsōsen*] the lowly. The hungry he as filled with good things; the rich he has sent away empty" (Luke 1:52-53; NABRE).

Isaiah also uses the Hebrew term *gābah* in speaking about the servant of the Lord. "See, my servant shall prosper, he shall be raised high and greatly exalted" (Isa 52:13; NABRE). In this example, the image of exaltation is coupled with "raise high," the Hebrew term *nāśāʾ*, which means to lift up something or someone. As seen here, the term *nāśāʾ* by extension can also mean to raise one's status or to exalt. These Hebrew terms are used widely in the OT. Interestingly, the Aramaic equivalent *ʾzdqyp*, "to be exalted," can also mean "to be crucified or hanged,"[45] which provides rich fodder for New Testament authors as we shall see below. When applied to Jesus, the metaphor of exaltation is meant to convey that Jesus' status has been raised by God.

[43] John 3:14; 8:28; 12:32-34; Acts 2:33; 5:31; Phil 2:9.
[44] BDB, s.v. *gābah*.
[45] BDAG, s.v. *hypsoō*.

The New Testament Greek term that conveys the sense of exaltation is *hypsoō*, the same term we saw in Luke 1:52. The verb has the basic sense of "lift up." It belongs to a class of verb that "makes" the noun from which it is based. The Greek Dictionary BDAG lists the noun *hypsos* as meaning (1) an "extent or distance upward, height"; (2) "a position of high status"; or (3) "lofty opinion of oneself." Thus the verb means (1) "to lift up spatially, *lift up, raise high*"; (2) "to cause enhancement in honor, fame, position, power, or fortune, *exalt*."[46]

The Greek verb is used with the first sense in the Gospel of John with a reference to Moses lifting up the serpent (John 3:14) and in the second sense in the LXX where God exalts or enhances one's honor (Ezek 21:31; Isa 52:13). There is much room for wordplay with this term, and that is not lost on the New Testament master of wordplay and irony, the author of the Gospel of John.

In the New Testament, the Gospel of John plays on the double meaning of lifted up (3:14; 8:28; 12:32) on the cross and/or lifted up in the sense of being exalted. For the author of John, the lifting up of Jesus:

> refers to one continuous act of ascent: Jesus begins his return to his Father as he approaches death (xiii 1) and completes it only with his ascension (xx 17). It is the upward swing of the great pendulum of the Incarnation corresponding to the descent of the Word which became flesh. The first step in the ascent is when Jesus is lifted up on the cross; the second step is when he is raised up from death; the final step is when he is lifted up to heaven. This wider understanding of "being lifted up" explains a statement like viii 28: "When you lift up the Son of Man, you will realize that I AM."[47]

Other New Testament authors will use "lifted up," but none use it quite as John does. For example, Acts 2:33 (*hypsōtheis*) and 5:32 together convey an image closely aligned to that of being seated at God's right hand.

Finally, the term is used in the great Christological hymn preserved in Paul's letter to the Philippians. Scholars long ago recognized Philippians 2:6-11 as a hymn. Though the precise date of Philippians is debated, there is general consensus that the letter was written in the late 50s CE. If the hymn has an Aramaic background as Fitzmyer

---

[46] Ibid., s.v. "*hypsos,*" "*hypsoō.*"
[47] Brown, *John,* vol. 1, 146.

suggests,[48] it does not seem implausible to propose that its origins may reach to Palestine from the 30s.

> Who, though he was in the form of God,
> did not regard equality with God something to be grasped.
> Rather, he emptied himself,
> taking the form of a slave,
> coming in human likeness;
> and found human in appearance,
> he humbled himself,
> becoming obedient to death, even death on a cross.
>
> Because of this, God greatly exalted [*hyperupsōsen*] him
> and bestowed on him the name
> that is above every name,
> that at the name of Jesus
> every knee should bend,
> of those in heaven and on earth and under the earth,
> and every tongue confess that
> Jesus Christ is Lord,
> to the glory of God the Father. (Phil 2:6-11; NABRE)

One looks to the Philippian hymn in vain for a mention of resurrection. Instead there is only the term "greatly exalted" (*hyperupsōsen*, Phil 2:9) to refer to Christ after death.[49]

The hymn is generally divided into two parts. The first deals with the lowliness and humility of Jesus. It begins with a relative clause, whose pronoun refers back to "Christ Jesus" in verse 5. Thus, Jesus is the subject of each verb in the first part of the hymn. The second part of the hymn has to do with exaltation. In this part, God is the subject of each verb. Scholars have done significant work on these few verses that we are not able to explore in detail here.[50] For our purposes, we note the use of "exaltation" rather than "resurrection" language in the hymn. That the hymn is early, dating from perhaps the first decade after the death of Jesus, is also significant. One of the

---

[48] J. A. Fitzmyer, "The Aramaic Background of Philippians 2:6-11," *CBQ* 3 (1988): 470–84.

[49] The term is used in 2 Corinthians 11:7 but not related to the exaltation of Jesus.

[50] E.g. Fitzmyer, "The Aramaic Background."

ways the earliest Palestinian "Christians" referred to what happened to Jesus after his death is by the term "exaltation." Indeed, this time period is so proximate to the death of Jesus that these followers were not yet known by the term "Christians."

In conclusion, the image of exaltation / being lifted up conveys the idea that Jesus has been given honor by God. Though the primary meaning of "lifted up" certainly connotes a thing being lifted into the air, the extended meaning "exalted" does not necessarily imply this spatial or physical sense. "To exalt" means simply "to give honor." Therefore, a potential weakness of this image is that it leaves aside the question of "what happened to the corpse" of Jesus. That Jesus after his death was exalted, or given honor by God, does not necessarily imply the corpse was raised. A positive reading of this image may remind us that what happened to Jesus' corpse may not have been a primary concern to the earliest Christians. For them, of primary importance was that God had reversed the shame of the cross and given Jesus the status of honor.

Glorified / Taken Up in Glory

Many times in the New Testament, authors will speak of Jesus entering glory, being glorified, or being taken up in glory.[51] Some of these images may overlap somewhat with exaltation, but the term common to the set of images now under consideration is "glory." Glory is an inanimate, intangible thing, hardly a substance that could be touched or felt. Glory (in Hebrew *kābôd*; in Greek *doxa*) is used in the Old Testament for the manifestation of Yahweh's presence (Exod 14:4, 17-18; 16:7, 10; 24:16; 40:34-35; Lev 9:6; Deut 5:24; Ps 18:1; 26:8; 72:19). Glory is also used in the Old Testament to convey something of an eschatological sense (Isa 43:7; 58:8; 60:1-2); glory is the image used to speak of the presence of God associated with the end times:

> Arise! Shine, for your light has come,
> the glory of the LORD has dawned upon you.
> Though darkness covers the earth,
> and thick clouds, the peoples,
> Upon you the LORD will dawn,
> and over you his glory will be seen (Isa 60:1-2; NABRE).

---

[51] Luke 24:26; John 7:39; 12:16, 23; 16:14; 17:4-5; Acts 3:13; Rom 8:17; Phil 3:21; Heb 2:7, 9; 1 Tim 3:16; 1 Pet 1:21; 2 Pet 1:17.

More than any other New Testament book, the Gospel of John uses the image of glory with respect to Jesus after his death. More often even than "resurrection," John uses the image of "glory." All of the uses in the Gospel of John are prior to Jesus' death, speaking of his coming glorification. For example, "but when Jesus was glorified, then they [the disciples] remembered that these things had been written of him and had been done to him" (John 12:16). By speaking only of the future glorification, John is different than Luke as we will see below.

Luke and Paul also use the term "glory" when speaking of the risen Christ. When Luke uses the term (Luke 24:26), we hear it on the lips of Jesus himself on the road to Emmaus: "Was it not necessary that the Messiah should suffer these things and enter into his glory?" (NABRE).[52] In this case, Jesus is speaking to the disciples as one who has already entered "glory." Jesus is appearing from glory. Thus, between the time of his death and the time he is speaking to the disciples on the road to Emmaus, Jesus has already enjoyed the radiant presence of God. It is from this presence that he appeared to the disciples according to Luke's presentation of the event.

For his part, Paul claims that Christ has been glorified (Rom 8:17) and raised by the glory of the Father (Rom 6:4). Paul speaks too of the glory of Christ (2 Cor 4:4; 8:23) and calls Christ the Lord of Glory (1 Cor 2:8). Paul claims that Christ's existence was of a heavenly realm. Thus, Christ himself possesses the glory of God. Paul also speaks of the body of Christ's glory (Phil 3:21). By predicating the term "glory" of body, Paul conveys its posttransformational presence with God. Christ's body has been transformed after death so that Christ now enjoys the presence of God and his glory.[53] The element of transformation is key to Paul's anthropological eschatology (e.g., 1 Cor 15:50).

L. T. Johnson cites the following Pauline passages when he makes the claim that "[glory] is used in the NT as the fundamental symbol for the resurrection of Jesus (Rom 6:4; 1 Cor 2:8; 15:43; 2 Cor 3:18; 4:4, 6; Phil 2:11)."[54] In discussing Paul's use of "taken up in glory" in

[52] We will neglect the question of the necessity of the suffering Messiah, a uniquely Lukan idea, which is beyond the scope of this study.

[53] B. Schmisek, "The Body of His Glory: Resurrection Imagery in Philippians 3:20-21" *BTB* 43, no. 1 (2013): 23–28.

[54] L. T. Johnson, *The First and Second Letters to Timothy*, AB 35A (New York: Doubleday, 2001), 234.

1 Timothy 3:16 (which Johnson takes to be an authentically Pauline letter), Johnson sees in this passage a use closer to the ascension language of Mark 16:9 and Luke–Acts. The passage would mean that Jesus has been taken up to share in the divine presence of God.

The only passage in the New Testament that explicitly links God's raising Jesus with giving him glory is 1 Peter 1:21: "[God] raised him from the dead and gave him glory." Elliott sees here an echo of LXX Isaiah 52:13, "Behold, my servant shall prosper and shall be exalted and greatly glorified."[55] In any case, the image of glory is meant to convey what it does in other New Testament texts. Jesus now enjoys the radiant divine presence.

Another unique case is 2 Peter 1:17, where the author says of Jesus, "he received honor and glory from God the Father when that unique declaration came to him from the majestic glory, 'This is my Son, my beloved, with whom I am well pleased'" (NABRE). Many commentators, as well as the notes from the NAB, link this episode to the transfiguration (Matthew 17:1-8 and parallels). Some influential scholars posit that the transfiguration itself is a displaced resurrection narrative, though not all share this view.[56] If the transfiguration is a version of a resurrection story, then the reception of "honor and glory" is another way of referring to the status of the risen Jesus.

A weakness of the "glory" metaphor is that when it is linked to "body" in Philippians 3:21, theologians and others have proposed fantastic theories such as ethereal bodies of light to explain the term "body of glory." So even though the term "glory" itself may not conjure up any physical notion, once it becomes an attribute of "body," the imagination becomes easily drawn to the earth once again. On a positive note, "glory" language gives one the sense of another realm.

---

[55] J. H. Elliott, *1 Peter*, AB 37B (New York: Doubleday, 2000), 378.

[56] Perhaps the most influential voice in favor of interpreting the transfiguration as a displaced resurrection narrative is R. Bultmann, *History of the Synoptic Tradition*, rev. ed. (New York: Harper & Row, 1963), 259. He is followed by C. E. Carlston, "Transfiguration and Resurrection," *JBL* 80 (1961): 233-40 and James M. Robinson, "Jesus: From Easter to Valentinus (or the Apostles' Creed)," *JBL* 101 (1982): 8-9, among others. Opposing views are articulated strongly by C. H. Dodd, "The Appearance of the Risen Christ: An Essay in Form Criticism of the Gospels" in *Studies in the Gospels*, ed. D. E. Nineham (Oxford, 1955): 9-35.

Glory connotes eschatology and the presence of the Lord. That Jesus shares in that presence now gives promise to the hope of the end times when we, like him, shall all share in the presence of God.

Ascension

The very graphic image of going up or being taken/carried up is found in Luke, Acts, the longer ending of Mark, 1 Timothy, and John.[57] The image is one of literal ascension and hearkens back to the story of 2 Kings wherein Elijah is taken to heaven. His return, which is associated with the coming victory of God, is awaited (e.g., Mal 3:23-24). In 2 Kings the Hebrew verb is *'lh* (meaning "go up, climb, or ascend") and is translated by the Greek verb *anelēmphthē* (LXX 2 Kings 2:11c), as in "Elijah was taken up [*anelēmphthē*] in a whirlwind into heaven."

Anelēmphthē is the passive form of the verb *analambanein* ("taken up"), which is used in Acts 1:2, 11, 22, and which echoes the passive form *anephereto*, "was carried up," in Luke 24:51. The term is equivalent to *epērēthē*, "was lifted up," in Acts 1:9, 1 Timothy 3:16, and Mark 16:19. Commentators will note that this is a use of the divine passive, which means God is the agent of the verb. In other words, "was carried up [by God]" or "was taken up [by God]." Active voice verbs are also used such as *anabainō*, "go up," in John 20:17 and *anebē*, "he went up," in Ephesians 4:9. We can see that there are a variety of Greek terms masked by the singular English term "ascension."

The graphic imagery of "being taken up" conveys the idea that after his death, Jesus was taken up into the realm of God, by God himself. Of course, this metaphor is based on an ancient cosmology that believed heaven was above the earth. Thus, to go to heaven one must go up. Fitzmyer recognizes that the ascension is Luke's "way of referring to what other (and earlier) New Testament writers have called Christ's 'exaltation' . . . Luke has dramatized the exaltation as a visibly perceptible ascension of Christ into heaven."[58] The image also implies, by a passive verb form, that God himself is the agent of Jesus' going up;

[57] Mark 16:9; Luke 24:51; John 20:17; Acts 1:2, 9, 11, 22; 1 Tim 3:16; cf. Eph 4:8.

[58] Joseph A. Fitzmyer, *Acts of the Apostles*, AB 18C (New York: Doubleday, 1998), 194.

his ascension was an act of God. Recall that one weakness we noted with the metaphor of exaltation is that it does not necessarily imply a physical body. Jesus can be exalted, or given honor by God, after his death without any reference to the corpse. By dramatizing the exaltation as a more literal ascension and in keeping with his tendency to objectivize the supernatural, Luke has made the action visibly perceptible.

In John 20:17 we have the unique case of the risen Jesus saying to Mary Magdalene, "Do not cling to me. I have not yet ascended [*anabebēka*] to my Father. But go to my brothers and tell them, 'I am ascending [*anabainō*] to my Father and your Father, my God and your God" (translation mine). This is unique in that Jesus speaks of ascending in the present tense. "The present tense here means that Jesus is already in the process of ascending but has not yet reached his final destination."[59] There is also the "futuristic use of the present" in which case a verb of coming or going can have the meaning of "to be in the process of going (coming)" for which reaching the destination still lies in the future.[60] That certainly appears to be the sense in this case as the ascension will take place before the next scene, which is Jesus' appearance to the disciples sans Thomas. The language of ascension in John echoes Jesus' earlier pronouncements about "going to the Father" (7:33; 14:12, 28; 16:5, 10, 28). By using the verb in the active voice (20:17), John emphasizes his high Christology, a staple of his gospel.[61] In John, Jesus is not taken up; rather, he ascends on his own power, by his own agency, for he is the Word that was with God, was made incarnate, and is returning to the Father (as we shall explore in more detail below).

The ascension metaphor implicitly answers the question about what happened to Jesus' body. For that reason some may find the image to be a strength. That is, the body of Jesus is in heaven for Jesus himself was lifted up into heaven. A weakness of this image is that the modern reader no longer accepts the cosmology of the ancient world. We realize that heaven is not "up," simply above the clouds. We know that the earth is a sphere and it orbits the sun. By going up above the clouds one enters not heaven but the stratosphere, the

---

[59] Brown, *John*, 994.

[60] BDF para. 323, no. 3.

[61] The term *anabainein*, "to ascend" or "to go up," becomes the predominant creedal term in early Christianity.

exosphere, and finally outer space. The literalism of the metaphor may have been a strength in antiquity but the modern reader may find it distracting.

Going to the Father / Him Who Sent Me

A predominantly Johannine image used throughout his gospel is "going to the Father." In one passage it is preceded by, "I am leaving the world and going to the Father" (16:28). In the Gospel of John there is a grand Christological arc: the Word was with God (1:1), became flesh (1:14), then returns to the Father (John 7:33; 13:1; 14:12, 28; 16:5, 10, 17, 28).

There are different Greek words used to convey "to go" such as *hypagein* (7:33; 16:5, 10) *aphienai* (leaving [the world], 16:28) and *poreuesthai* (14:12, 28; 16:28). The variation in terms to express essentially the same thing is typically Johannine.[62] The words simply mean "go" in the sense of journey or walk. In terms of Johannine theology, Jesus was with the Father and he will be returning to the Father.

A strength of this metaphor is that it emphasizes a return. This is part of the Christological arc of the Gospel of John; namely, the Word was with God, the Word became flesh, then returns to the Father. Another strength is that this metaphor often occurs with sayings like, "In my Father's house there are many dwelling places. If there were not, would I have told you that I am going to prepare a place for you? And if I go and prepare a place for you, I will come back again and take you to myself, so that where I am you also may be" (John 14:2-3; NABRE). Of course, John does not understand Jesus as literally making a place or home in heaven but the image conveys the communal aspect of salvation, similar to what Paul expressed when he said, "we shall always be with the Lord" (1 Thess 4:17b; NABRE). So, there is a soteriological dimension to Jesus' return to the Father. Jesus returns to the Father so we too can be with the Father and with Jesus. A potential negative of this metaphor is that when it is combined with the saying about preparing a place, it can easily be interpreted literally.

---

[62] For example, John uses both *agapāo* and *phileō* to express "love" without any apparent distinction in meaning.

Vindicated in the Spirit

At this point in our review of metaphors, we have examined the most prominent: resurrection, exaltation, glorification, and ascension. What remain now are metaphors used less frequently, though they are not less important.

One metaphor unique in all the New Testament is that found in 1 Timothy 3:16: vindicated or justified in the spirit. For more than one hundred years, scholars have recognized that 1 Timothy 3:16 seems to preserve a hymn, like Philippians 2:6-11 and Colossians 1:15-20. Like Philippians and Colossians, the 1 Timothy hymn begins with a relative pronoun that refers to Christ. The phrases are balanced and rhymes have been noted.

Who	was manifested in the flesh	*hos*	*ephanerōthē en sarki*
	Vindicated by the spirit		*edikaiōthē en pneumati*
	Appeared to messengers		*ōphthē angelois*
	Preached among the nations		*ekēruchthē en ethnesin*
	Believed in by the world		*episteuthē en kosmō[i]*
	Taken up in glory		*anelēmphthē en doxē[i]*[63]

The phrase that concerns us here is the second of the hymn: "vindicated by the spirit," which seems to balance the first, "manifested in the flesh." Of course, flesh and spirit are favorite Pauline opposites. Whether or not Paul wrote 1 Timothy, the Pauline penchant for these oppositions is clear.[64] The contrast is not only between flesh and spirit but also between *manifested* and *vindicated*. In this way, the contrast is similar to that in Romans 1:3-4:

[who was] born from the seed of David	*tou genomenou ek spermatos Dauid*
according to the flesh,	*kata sarka*
but established as son of God in power	*tou horisthentos huiou theou en dunamei*
according to a spirit of holiness,	*kata pneuma hagiōsunēs*
as of his resurrection from the dead.	*ex anastaseōs nekrōn*[65]

---

[63] N-A[27]

[64] Paul often juxtaposes flesh and spirit—e.g., Romans 8:1-13 and Galatians 5:16-25. This is the only use of *sarx* (flesh) in the deutero-Pauline corpus.

[65] N-A[27]

In Romans the contrast is between *born* and *established, seed of David* and *son of God in power*, and *according to the flesh* and *according to a spirit of holiness*. The distinction in Romans and in 1 Timothy is between his earthly and heavenly life, or as L. T. Johnson puts it, "between his human appearance and his exaltation by resurrection."[66]

The verb that means "to vindicate," "to justify," or "to make righteous" is *dikaioō*. Like *hypsoō* (to lift up/exalt), this is an omicron contract verb, denoting a factitive sense. The verb *dikaioō* "makes" the noun from which it is based. The Greek noun *dikaios* means "just" or "righteous," so *dikaoō* means "to make just," "to make righteous," or "to vindicate." Romans 4:2 is an example of the verb carrying the sense of "vindicate." Most often however, the translation of this term into English is complicated by the reformation debates surrounding "justification by faith." But in 1 Timothy 3:16, these debates are not at issue. Instead, 1 Timothy 3:16 means that after Jesus' earthly life he was vindicated or made righteous by the spirit of God. Jesus was made to stand in a right relationship with God by the agency of God's spirit. That Paul saw the spirit as the agent of Christ's resurrection is clear from Romans 1:4; 8:2; 15:19; 1 Corinthians 12:3; 15:45; and 2 Corinthians 3:17.

Perhaps one weakness in the image is that it may lead to questioning whether Jesus was righteous or "stood in a right relationship" with God prior to his death. One would suppose that Jesus was in a right relationship with God throughout his entire life. So this passage may leave open an adoptionist interpretation, which would claim that, at some point after his death, God bestowed on Jesus the status of son, thereby "adopting" him. Classical or orthodox Christology would hold that Jesus was son of God throughout his entire life. But adoptionist tendencies are found in other parts of the New Testament. For example, Acts of the Apostles seems to preserve an ancient speech or early kerygma in which Jesus is "made both Lord and Messiah" after his death (2:36). Here too, orthodox Christology would maintain that Jesus was Lord and Messiah throughout his entire life. These were not titles bestowed on him as a reward after death. Such inklings of adoptionism in the New Testament give scholars the notion that these texts preserve early kerygma. The primitive

---

[66] L. T. Johnson, *First and Second Letters to Timothy*, 233.

Christological hymn of 1 Timothy 3:16 would be an example of such an early kerygma that saw vindication happening after death. So the weakness of the image, that it is open to adoptionism, may also be a strength in that it preserves primitive material.

Another potential weakness with this metaphor is that there is no explicit mention of death. In the Philippians hymn for example, there is the mention of death in the phrase, "even death on a cross." In 1 Timothy, however, we find no mention of death. Also, 1 Timothy 3:16 is the only such use of "vindication" to speak of Christ's triumph over death. The image does not receive much attention. As a result, many modern Christians may simply be unfamiliar with this unique image.

In Paradise/Heaven

Paradise is used often in popular speech today as a synonym for heaven. The origin of the term is of the Old Persian word *pairidaêza*, meaning "enclosed space, precinct." It is transliterated into Greek as *paradeisos*. When the word is used by the pagan Greek author Xenophon (ca. 430–354 BCE), it means "enclosed space, garden." The Septuagint uses *paradeisos* to translate the Hebrew term for "garden" or "enclosure" (*gan*) in Genesis 2:8 and 2:15 in the phrase "garden of Eden" and again in Genesis 13:10, "the garden of the LORD." Thus, the term "paradise" used in the Old Testament began to carry eschatological notions (cf. Ezek 31:8). In extrabiblical literature[67] it came to mean "the mythical place or abode of the righteous after death" and thus its meaning in Luke.[68]

Other than Luke, the term is used only twice in the New Testament: 2 Corinthians 12:4 and Revelation 2:7. In the 2 Corinthians passage Paul speaks of a mystical vision of one caught up in "paradise." In Revelation 2:7 there is a reference to the tree of life in God's paradise (garden), echoing Genesis 2:9 and Ezekiel 31:8. The passage from Revelation reads, "to the victor I will give the right to eat from the tree of life that is in the garden (*paradeisos*) of God." So in each of the two cases, paradise has a nuanced meaning slightly different than "heaven," though it has often been reduced to an equivalent of that term. In each case, the term paradise means something closer to the "abode of the righteous after death."

---

[67] *T. Levi* 18:10-11; *Ps. Sol.* 14:3; *1 Enoch* 17-19; 60:8; 61:12.
[68] Fitzmyer, *Luke*, 1510–11.

In the Gospel of Luke, Jesus addresses the repentant thief with "Today you will be with me in paradise" (Luke 23:43). Thus, that very day Jesus is going to the mythical place reserved for the righteous after death. This place hearkens back to the garden of God, promised to those who are righteous. Jesus not only will be there immediately after his death but will have the power to bring others with him.

The image of Jesus in paradise may echo the Pauline notion of the risen Lord "in heaven" (Rom 10:6). As we have seen, for Paul, being with the Lord is the destination of believers: "We shall always be with the Lord" (1 Thess 4:17; NABRE) or "my desire is to depart [this life] and be with Christ, for that is far better" (Phil 1:23).

One weakness with the image of paradise is that, although modern people are familiar with the term, most know neither its background nor its association with the abode of the righteous. Instead, the term is often viewed simply as "heaven," in the sense of "realm of God." In reality, the term conveys much more than an ethereal place. Fortunately, many people are familiar with the image today, even if they do not fully know its background. For many, "paradise" conjures up the realm of God, if not the realm of the righteous who have died.

Entering the Holy of Holies

The image of Jesus Christ entering the holy of holies with his own blood (Heb 9:12, 24-26) is unique to Hebrews. Indeed much of the Letter to the Hebrews is *sui generis*. For our purposes, we simply draw attention to another image, this one wholly unique, to speak of Christ after his death.

The Old Testament background to this image is one of temple sacrifice and the Yom Kippur[69] ritual, celebrated each year on the tenth of Tishri (September–October) (Lev 16:1-19; 23:26-32; Num 29:7-11). To understand better the ritual it is helpful to remember that there were two sanctuaries in the temple: the outer sanctuary known as the "holy place" and the inner sanctuary known as the "holy of holies" (Exod 26:33-35), the earthly dwelling place of God's glory.

---

[69] Yom Kippur is a Hebrew term meaning Day of Atonement or Expiation. The *kappōret* (from which the term Kippur is derived) is the mercy seat, or covering, on the ark of the covenant where the ritual blood is placed, atoning for or expiating the sins of the people.

Priests were permitted in the holy place on a daily basis to perform ritual functions like burning incense (Exod 30:6-8), keeping olive oil supplied in the lamps (Exod 27:20-21), and replacing the showbread each Sabbath (Lev 24:8). Only the high priest could enter the holy of holies, and this only once each year on the feast of Yom Kippur (Lev 16:1-19).

The ritual of Yom Kippur performed by the high priest used the blood of a bull as a means of atoning for the high priest and his family (Lev 16:11). The high priest then slaughtered a goat, whose blood was used to atone for the sins of Israel. The blood of the goat was brought into the holy of holies and sprinkled on the *kappōret* (the cover of the ark), and sprinkled and rubbed on the altar (16:15-19). By means of this ritual the people were at one with God.

The author of Hebrews uses this imagery and reinterprets it in light of Christ. For the author of Hebrews, Jesus has entered the true holy of holies in heaven, the true dwelling place of God, not merely a copy on earth, so that Jesus might appear before God on our behalf (Heb 9:24). The blood Jesus offers is not that of a bull or a goat but his very own (Heb 9:12). There is no need for this to be repeated year after year as they do in the temple each Yom Kippur, for the sacrifice of Jesus is eternal. It takes away sin once and for all (Heb 9:24-26).

Thus, the author of Hebrews presents a unique image of an eternal heavenly Yom Kippur ritual with Jesus as high priest according to a Melchizedekian (rather than Levitical) priesthood. In fact, the Letter to the Hebrews has many features that are peculiar when speaking of Christ's exaltation. The word resurrection occurs only once in the letter (6:2). The image of resurrection is alluded to only once, near the end of the letter: "May the God of Peace, who, by the blood of an eternal covenant, led up from the dead the great shepherd of the sheep, our Lord Jesus" (Heb 13:20). Attridge believes that the avoidance of the term "raised up" in favor of "led up" is deliberate as Hebrews uses exaltation language rather than resurrection language.[70] The author does not change course in the few remaining verses (the last verse of the letter is 13:25). Other images are also keen in the mind of the author such as Christ's becoming High Priest (Heb 1:4; 6:20; 7:26)

---

[70] Harold Attridge, *Hebrews: A Commentary on the Epistle to the Hebrews*, Hermeneia (Minneapolis, MN: Fortress, 1989), 406.

or his becoming "perfected" (Heb 2:10; 5:9). These images are also unique to the Letter to the Hebrews.

One weakness of the image of Jesus entering the heavenly holy of holies is that it requires a familiarity with the Old Testament Temple and the feast of Yom Kippur. Unfortunately, many modern Christians are unfamiliar with Yom Kippur, not to mention other Jewish feasts. So, the image of Jesus presenting his own blood in the heavenly Temple, not made by human hands, as an expiation for sin once and for all, may not be readily apparent to those unfamiliar with Yom Kippur. On the other hand, a strength of this image is that it invites us to become more familiar with first-century thought. Moreover, the image is thoroughly and inextricably rooted in the Old Testament. When we recognize that there are metaphors unfamiliar to us but still pertinent for expressing faith, we might be encouraged to explore them, allowing us to have greater appreciation for the early Christian witness.

The Strength of Many Metaphors

In sum, resurrection is the predominant metaphor among many to speak of what happened to Christ after his death. But even resurrection is a metaphor. When the New Testament authors applied the metaphor to Jesus, they meant more than the raising of Jairus' daughter (Luke 8:54-55), the son of the widow of Nain (Luke 7:15), Lazarus (John 11:43-44; 12:1-2), or the widow's son who was raised by Elijah (1 Kings 17:17-24). Even in the resurrection narratives, Jesus appeared "in another form" (Mark 16:12; Luke 24:13-32). The risen Jesus is not merely a reanimated corpse (cf. Mark 6:14, 16). In each of the gospels, Jesus' own resurrection was something qualitatively different. Lazarus, Jairus's daughter, the son of the widow of Nain, and the son of the widow raised by Elijah all died at a later time. Jesus, once raised from the dead, is no longer subject to death. And as we mentioned earlier, the resurrection of Jesus transcends even the category of resurrection.

Thus we examine other metaphors. If we limit ourselves to only one we may develop a skewed notion of the mystery of Jesus' eternal life. We find that there are many New Testament metaphors to speak of the risen Lord. But each is just that: a metaphor. Jesus is not literally sitting in a chair next to God, but he enjoys the power and the status of God. Jesus is not literally lifted up into heaven above the clouds, but he is with God. Jesus is not literally in a garden, but he does enjoy the abode of the righteous. Jesus is not literally made of glory, but he does enjoy the radiant presence of God. Finally, Jesus, unlike Jairus' daughter, the son of the widow of Nain, or Lazarus, or the widow's son raised by Elijah, is not literally raised from the dead, but having conquered death, he is no longer subject to it.

Ultimately, there is no perfectly apt metaphor to speak of what happened to Jesus after he died. Perhaps this is why the early church used so many. Today, as we read the New Testament witness to the living Christ, it is as though we are looking at the Christ-event as a multisided gemstone. Each angle, each face gives us new insights. No one face or angle presents the gemstone in its entirety. For that we must rotate and examine the gemstone from various angles. In a similar way, the fundamental reality of what happened to Jesus after his death cannot be encapsulated in one image or one metaphor. We must step back, away from each metaphor in the hope that we will see something of the whole. By distancing ourselves from one metaphor to recognize another we may come to a deeper insight. By recognizing the plurality of images used by New Testament authors we may grasp something of the mystery of what the early church experienced. Once we recognize that no single metaphor can convey the mystery of Christ's exaltation in its entirety, will we be in a better place to convey the profundity of this fundamental mystery to the modern world.

Chapter 3

Our Vast Knowledge

We live in a postmodern era; we know more about the world and how it works than the ancients did. Yet the theological task, like that of our ancient forebears in faith, is to express Christianity in terms the modern culture can understand and find meaningful. Clement did this when he likened resurrection to a phoenix rising from its ashes. Justin Martyr, Irenaeus, and the apologists did this when they cast Christianity in terms of Greek philosophy and thus wedded body-soul anthropology with Christian faith. Augustine did this when he expressed Christian faith in terms of neoplatonic philosophy. Aquinas did this when he recast Christian faith in light of Aristotelian philosophy and the science of the thirteenth century. This is the enduring theological task: to cast Christian faith in the language, terms, and culture of the day. As the most recent document from the International Theological Commission states: "In language intelligible to every generation, she [the church] should be able to answer the ever recurring questions which (people) ask about the meaning of this present life and of the life to come, and how one is related to the other."[1] The commission insists upon "language intelligible to every generation." It is not sufficient merely to quote ancient formulas to modern people who do not share the philosophical presuppositions of the ancient world. We must tap into the fundamental beliefs of our forebears in faith and express that faith in language intelligible to our generation.

Our knowledge and understanding of the created world is vastly different than that of the ancient. For example, we understand the size, scale, and age of the universe in much different ways. We recognize

---

[1] TTPPC, 51.

that human beings are a product of evolution and that we share a great deal with the natural world and other living creatures. The list could go on and on, but for our purposes we shall sketch these two vast categories (the model of the universe and human beings) in broad strokes, colored by occasional vignettes and open-ended questions to provoke thought. This section is more akin to a basic review of what we in the modern world know about these subjects. The material will be familiar. The section may feel like a quick tour through a vast body of knowledge, barely stopping for interesting tidbits or curiosities. Bear with your "tour guide" for the following pages. After this general review we will examine how our understanding of resurrection might be affected by this knowledge.

Model of the Universe

Nongeocentricity

Perhaps one of the greatest differences between the ancient view of the world and the modern would be that we have discarded the notion of a geocentric universe. The ancient (biblical) view of the world imagined a fairly stable earth on pillars with a dome above it. God kept storehouses of rain, hail, and ice, for example, above the dome (cf. e.g., Deut 28:12; Job 38:22; Ps 135:7; Jer 10:13; 51:16). The moon, sun, and stars were set in the sky above the dome and followed the tracks established for them by God. They were made of ethereal matter, or something otherworldly. The biblical worldview is depicted rather well on a page from the Catholic Book Publishing edition of the New American Bible (see appendix B).

Today, we know that there are not storehouses of rain, sleet, and hail kept atop a dome that rests over the earth.

In the sixteenth century Galileo looked at the moon through a telescope that had the magnifying power equivalent to that of a ten-dollar pair of binoculars today. At his time the moon was thought to exist in the heavenly, ethereal realm and, therefore, be made of something ethereal.[2] After examining the moon through a telescope, Galileo pro-

---

[2] Even in the twentieth century scientists were devising experiments to test for the rarified ether. At that time it was thought that the ether was a thin material through which all matter in the universe moved. The theory of the ether's existence dissipated less than one hundred years ago.

posed that the moon was made of the same "stuff" as the earth, not some ethereal matter. This was a revolutionary idea. Yet today Galileo's idea is foundational to our understanding of the universe. Everything in the universe is made up of the same stuff, or *matter*, which itself is made up of atoms represented by the periodic table of elements.

Not only have we come to realize that all matter throughout the universe is made up of atoms, but we also understand that the earth, along with seven other planets, asteroids, comets, exoplanets, and other material, orbits the sun, a rather medium-sized yellow star on the edge of the Milky Way Galaxy. Orbits are established by the inter-action of a mass's gravity, a force that exists throughout the universe. With a geocentric universe it might be easy to believe that the earth is the center and focal point of creation. But we now know that the earth is simply one of many other planets in the solar system and one of many more that we know of in the galaxy. With the recent landing of the spacecraft Opportunity on Mars, many scientists are saying that the question is not whether we will find life beyond the earth but when. Like a child who learns a fundamental reality required for growth and development, only recently we learned to say and believe, "We are not the center of the universe." Any musings on resurrection and afterlife will need to take this notion into account.

Space

We now know the sun is not merely "in the sky" but that it is about ninety-three million miles away. With a diameter of a bit more than one hundred times that of earth, the sun's volume is more than a million times larger than the earth. We might be familiar with a distance of one hundred miles or even a thousand, but few of us can really imagine one million miles, much less ninety-three million miles. To grasp the immensity of the sizes and distances we are con-templating, we could scale this down to something more imaginable. If the sun were four inches in diameter, the earth would be the size of a grain of salt (about 1 millimeter) over thirty-five feet away. At that scale, Pluto would be more than a quarter mile away and the nearest star, Alpha Centauri, over eighteen hundred miles away. The center of our own galaxy would be nearly twelve million miles away, not to mention other galaxies. Even at that scale the distances are immense and nearly impossible to comprehend.

And now we know that aside from planets, not every object we see in the night sky is a star. There are countless other galaxies in the universe, each with hundreds of billions of stars. The immensity of the universe is simply overwhelming when we consider that our sun is one of billions in our own galaxy, and our galaxy is one of at least two hundred billion. Astronomers are now demonstrating that many of these suns have planets orbiting them, orbits that are determined by gravity. Finally, we also recognize that the universe is expanding exponentially. That is to say, galaxies farther away from us are moving away at a faster rate. It seems that the very fabric of space is being stretched. This was unknown to educated ancients and unknown even to the overwhelming majority of educated people of the nineteenth century. The sheer size of the universe may cause the modern Christian to wonder about his or her place in the world, life's meaning, and the possibility of afterlife.

Time

Through the centuries, human beings became better at measuring time, primarily in years, months, and days, but then later in even more refined ways such as hours, minutes, seconds, and nanoseconds. Until recently (the past one hundred years or so), we thought time was a constant, ticking away at the same rate in all places everywhere. Today, we recognize that time is not constant, but interrelated to space such that physicists talk of the fabric of "space-time" or the space-time continuum. Albert Einstein developed this theory in the early twentieth century and it has now been confirmed many times by experiment. Like many before him, Einstein recognized our three dimensions of space: up-down; left-right; back-forth. It is possible to situate any object in the universe in these three dimensions. And we now have global positioning systems to help us with this! Einstein's genius was to posit time as a fourth dimension, interrelated to our three spatial dimensions.

To approach a better understanding of the interrelatedness of time and space, let's first discuss the interrelatedness of the three dimensions of space using airplanes as an example. If we imagine an airplane leaving Dallas heading due east at a velocity of six hundred miles per hour and another airplane leaving Dallas heading northeast at a velocity of six hundred miles per hour, which will make more easterly progress after one hour? The answer is simple and straightforward. The first airplane will make more easterly progress than the second because the second is also using its velocity to head north. The velocity of six hundred miles per hour can be "spent" in a number of directions or combinations thereof: north, south, east, west, or even in altitude. The three dimensions of space are interrelated.

Using Einstein's insight, and later proof, that space and time are likewise related, we now know that the faster an object travels through space, the less energy it "spends" moving through time. As an airplane heading due east makes more easterly progress than the airplane heading northeast, an object heading through space with great velocity makes more progress through space and spends less energy moving through time. Thus, we say time "slows down" for an object approaching the speed of light (about 186,000 miles/second). Even at six hundred miles per hour—equivalent to ten miles per minute or 0.167 miles per second—an object spends energy moving through time. An airplane would have to travel one million times faster than that and still it would not be traveling at the speed of light. So even though six hundred miles per hour may seem fast, and energy is spent moving through time as well as space, so little energy is spent moving through time (when compared to 186,000 miles/second), that the effect on time for that object is negligible.

So no longer do we think of time as a constant. Instead, the rate time passes is related to motion. Recognizing that space and time are different but related aspects of the same fabric of reality may cause us to imagine resurrection or the afterlife in a different way. Indeed, we are so deeply embedded in a seemingly constant world of space-time, it might seem impossible to imagine a life outside that reality.

Multidimensionality

In addition to recognizing that time is a dimension, some physicists are proposing even more dimensions to our physical world. The multidimensional theories are based on the physics of subatomic particles, or quantum mechanics and a desire to "connect" the math of subatomic particles to the theory of general relativity discussed above. For the mathematics to work, at least ten dimensions are postulated; that is to say, in order to describe mathematically everything from the smallest particle to the largest structure of the universe, physicists propose multidimensionality. While these theories have yet to be proven, much of the evidence points in this direction.

Perhaps it is not so difficult to imagine a world with dimensions we cannot perceive. In fact, when we consider the visible spectrum, we know that there are waves we cannot perceive — namely infrared and ultraviolet. Though our eyes do not naturally perceive these wavelengths, they certainly exist. To detect infrared and ultraviolet, we have developed scientific instruments from heat sensors to telescopes, all of which give us an even better understanding of the universe. Maybe in the not-to-distant future, scientific instruments, like the particle accelerator in Europe, will detect the existence of multidimensions.

As we conclude this brief section we might ask how this model of the universe, its non-geocentricity, its vastness, the interrelationship between space and time, and the possibility of multi-dimensionality affect our theology, especially our understanding of life after death. We shall keep these thoughts ruminating while we proceed to explore more aspects of the modern view of the world.

Age of the Universe

Scientists believe the universe is about 13.7 billion years old. This is a staggering number. Just look at it: 13,700,000,000. Our earth is thought to be about 4.556 billion years old with anaerobic bacteria having appeared on the earth about 4.2–3.8 billion years ago. Not until about three billion years later (or 550 million years ago) did multicellular organisms with hard parts appear on the earth. Life then exploded on earth, diversifying and inhabiting every nook and cranny on the land and under the sea.

Between the origin of the multicellular organism and the major species radiation (expansion of species in variety and places) of the mammals about fifty million years ago, the proliferation of life has experienced five mass extinctions.[3] After each of these five mass extinctions, life continued to proliferate. That is, many new species developed after each of the extinctions. Biologists, geologists, paleon-

---

[3] Ordovician 430 mya, Devonian 350 mya, Permian 225 mya, Triassic 200 mya, Cretaceous 65 mya (besides smaller events). Richard Leakey and Roger Lewin, *Origins Reconsidered: In Search of What Makes Us Human* (New York: Doubleday, 1992), 354.

tologists, and other scientists have devised a system of classification to speak of the various eras, periods, and epochs in earth's history. Most of us memorized some form of the chart that follows in middle school. It helps us speak of the different ages of the earth.

Cosmic Calendar

Carl Sagan, an astronomer with a gift for popularization, illustrated the infinitesimal amount of time we humans have been here by using the "cosmic calendar." That is, the entire 13.7 billion year history of the universe is compressed to one year. One month represents a bit more than one billion years; each minute, thirty thousand years; each second, five hundred years.

On this scale, the big bang happened at midnight on January 1. The Milky Way Galaxy was formed sometime in May. The earth was formed about mid-October. Mammals began their rise on December 30. All of written human history, (seventy-five hundred years) occurred in the last fifteen seconds of December 31. The cosmic calendar helps us realize how recently we humans appeared on the scene of the universe.

The chart below illustrates the major eras, periods, and some epochs in the life of the earth, with their relative dating on the cosmic calendar. There is naturally some debate about when each era or period begins and ends. Different charts use slightly different dates. As scientists continue to gather new data, the dates become more refined.

The sheer age of the universe, like its size, may cause the modern Christian to wonder about meaning. We no longer hold beliefs, as articulated by Justin Martyr or Irenaeus, that the earth is six thousand years old, created according to Genesis 1. It might be easy to believe that the earth is the center and focal point of creation, with humanity as its purpose, if like the ancients we subscribed to a young, geocentric universe, whose pinnacle creation (humanity) was made directly by God. But our modern knowledge indicates otherwise. The earth is much older than the ancients imagined; humanity only recently "arrived" on the scene.

One possible response to this body of scientific evidence is to dismiss it (e.g., creationists). But there are other, more plausible responses that respect the sphere of knowledge that science commands. By recognizing the age, expanse, and vastness of the universe, one need not deny God. The task of the theologian is to present God in terms that embrace this fundamental view of reality rather than deny it. Many theologians

Cosmic Calendar	Era	Period	Million Years Ago
		Quaternary	Holocene epoch
Dec 31, 11:59:40 p.m.			0.01
	Cenozoic	Quaternary	Pleistocene epoch
			2.6
		Neogene	
			26
		Paleogene	
Dec 30 noon			65
		Cretaceous	
Dec 29	Mesozoic		138
		Jurassic	
Dec 27			200
		Triassic	
Dec 26			225
		Permian	
Dec 25	Paleozoic		290
		Carboniferous	
Dec 24			350
		Devonian	
Dec 23			410
		Silurian	
Dec 22			430
		Ordovician	
Dec 21			505
		Cambrian	
Dec 18			550
	Proterozoic		
November 1			2500
October	Archean		

have engaged this pursuit. Before we look to the fruit of their labor, let us examine in more detail some insights from the modern world.

Human Beings

We have seen that it is possible to imagine the human being in ways other than "body and soul." Indeed, we have seen that this is the case in the vast majority of the biblical witness. Christian theology need not be wedded to a Platonic or Aristotelian anthropological system. Today, biologists and psychologists do not use "soul" or "breath of life" to differentiate a living from a nonliving thing. Instead, they apply the term "living" to an organism that is capable of growth and reproduction. A living organism consumes nutrients and passes waste.

Is it possible to speak of the human person without using the philosophical concept "soul"? Can one still be Christian without expressing the human being in terms of body and soul? Neither Jesus nor the apostles would have used those terms. Perhaps we might pursue a way to speak about the human being without retaining ancient Greek philosophical categories that no longer seem to speak to the modern world. What do scientists use to speak of human beings? What is a human being? What makes us human? The question sounds simple but a satisfying answer can be elusive.

Anthropology and Evolution

Charles Darwin published *On the Origin of the Species by Means of Natural Selection* in 1859. The book lit a firestorm in many quarters, especially theology. The effect of this theory appeared to diminish the role of God in the world. Darwin's theory proposed a creation that was driven not by divine purpose, but by randomness, chance, and the law of the jungle—a fierce "kill or be killed" understanding of nature. Human beings were not creatures made directly by God six thousand years ago; instead, they were understood to be closely related to apes! Even today, more than one hundred fifty years after the publication of the book, when scientists throughout the world have accepted Darwin's basic thesis, theologians are still grappling with the effect of his ideas. As with the age of the universe, there are two basic responses to Darwin's theories: dismissal or acceptance. We shall attempt the latter.

It was only seven million years ago that bipedal creatures began to walk upright. Anthropologists believe human consciousness arose about 2.5 million years ago. *Homo sapiens* (modern humans) appeared about forty thousand years ago. One might suggest that an individual of the species *Homo sapiens* is a human.

Insights into the nature of humanity might come from such a simple task as classifying human beings vis-á-vis other living things. This science, with its roots in antiquity, is known as taxonomy: the naming and classifying of species. Today the classic seven categories of kingdom, phylum, class, order, family, genus, and species are subdivided further. For our purposes, we will use the classic categories for the taxonomy of *Homo sapiens*.

Kingdom:	Animalia
Phylum:	Chordata
Class:	Mammalia (skin with hair, nourished by milk-secreting glands of adult)
Order:	Primates (large brains, stereoscopic vision, walking on two or four limbs)
Family:	Hominidae (Chimpanzees, Orangutans, Gorillas, Humans)
Genus:	*Homo*
Species:	*sapiens*

As one clearly sees, the genus *Homo* is part of the family *Hominidae* that also includes chimpanzees, orangutans, and gorillas. As such, the term hominid most often today refers to great apes and humans. The *Homo sapiens* is, in fact, the only species remaining in the genus *Homo*. All other species in the genus are extinct. Perhaps this is part of the reason why we humans think of ourselves as unique on the earth, somehow inevitable, and the very purpose of creation.

Biological taxonomy differentiates *Homo sapiens* from other species in the family hominid by physical characteristics, but there are unique behavioral and social characteristics, too. *Homo sapiens* have large brains relative to their size. The cerebral cortex itself is large and gives the human being capacity for language acquisition and expression, and high degrees of cognitive ability.

Some anthropologists will extend the meaning of the term human to include "apes that walked upright."[4] Such a definition reaches

---

[4] Richard Leakey, *The Origin of Humankind* (New York: Harper Collins, 1994), xiii.

back in time to include bipedal creatures who lived seven million years ago with brain sizes of about 450 to 600 cubic centimeters. These creatures and their related species were distinguished from other species precisely because of their upright walk. They still had small brains, funnel-shaped chests, and no waists. From these early bipedal creatures evolved the earliest hominid species (of the family *hominidae*) known as *Australopithecus afarensis*, who lived about 3.4 million years ago. The origin of the genus *Homo* was about 2.5 million years ago with the emergence of *Homo habilis* (handy man, or the species that first used tools). The average brain size of *Homo habilis* was about 800 cubic centimeters. *Homo erectus* (erect man) arrived about two million years ago with a larger brain, and the ability to hunt, run, and use fire. The early *Homo erectus* brains were about 900 cubic centimeters. In terms of longevity, this was the most successful species of *Homo*, leaving a fossil record of over one million years.

The evolution of *Homo sapiens* is debated fiercely. Anthropologists and other scientists continually are finding more fossils, learning more, and testing theories about precisely how our species evolved. The fossil record is not as complete as we would like. So, in addition to anthropologists, geneticists have applied their knowledge to the question of human origins. A complete picture is yet to emerge. For our purposes, we shall use broad strokes in generally agreed upon statements to paint this picture.

Homo sapiens evolved from earlier *Homo* species by showing skills with language, art, and technological innovation — that is, the ability to use tools and toolkits. *Homo heidelbergensis* seems to have been the common ancestor to both *Homo sapiens* and *Homo Neanderthalensis* (man from the Neander Valley; now commonly referred to as *Neanderthal*).[5]

Various *Homo* species would have mastered fire about seven hundred thousand years ago, in the Paleolithic age. The genetic split between the predecessors of Neanderthals and *Homo sapiens* would have occurred between four and seven hundred thousand years ago. DNA mitochondrial evidence indicates that *Homo sapiens* became a truly

---

[5] Though the first fossils were found in the Neander Valley, others have since been found across Europe (south of the Neander Valley) and into modern-day Israel, Syria, Iraq and as far east as Uzbekistan. Chris Stringer and Peter Andrews, *The Complete World of Human Evolution* (New York: Thames & Hudson, 2005), 156.

distinct species among others about one to two hundred thousand years ago in Africa.[6] This evidence reveals that all modern human beings share a common genetic ancestor referred to as "mitochondrial Eve" or "Africa Eve." *Homo sapiens* then migrated from Africa, eventually inhabiting most of the earth. About forty thousand years ago the modern human emerged. Neanderthals would have shared the planet with *Homo sapiens* until about twenty-eight thousand years ago, when Neanderthals died out.[7] There is evidence that Neanderthals had been using fire, making cave paintings, and burying their dead. After the extinction of Neanderthals, *Homo sapiens* became the sole surviving species of the genus *Homo*. More modern *Homo sapiens* developed agricultural techniques about ten thousand years ago in the Mesolithic age, the skill of writing about five thousand years ago or more in the Late Neolithic / Early Bronze age. About that time, human beings began forging bronze (by melting copper and tin together); two thousand years later, the Iron Age began.

In the past five thousand years, humanity has shaped the environment more than we have been shaped by it. In fact, some anthropologists believe we have altered our environment to such a degree that we have entered a new epoch in the geological time scale: anthropocene.

Returning to our cosmic calendar, and incorporating the commonly used "age" system for identifying periods in ancient human history, we can see just how recently these events occurred on a grand scale. Nearly every item on the chart takes place during the last hour of the last day of the year.

We recognize now how connected we are to other species in the world. Human DNA and chimpanzee DNA is 97.5 percent similar. Human DNA and Neanderthal DNA have even more in common. Human emergence was gradual, not sudden. What the fossil record showed us last century, the molecular or DNA record is confirming for us today. Yet, a major characteristic distinguishing humanity from other species is the sheer size of the human brain, especially in relation to our size.

---

[6] Jonathan Lunine, *Earth: Evolution of a Habitable World,* Cambridge Atmospheric and Space Science Series (Cambridge: Cambridge University Press, 1998), 260.

[7] Stephen S. Hall, "Last of the Neanderthals: Why Did Our Ice Age Rivals Vanish?" *National Geographic* 214, no. 4 (October 2008): 58.

Cosmic Calendar Dec 31	Epoch		Age		Time
11:59:55 p.m.	Holocene (or Anthropocene)				586 BCE
			Iron Age		
11:59:54 p.m.					1,200 BCE
			Bronze Age		
11:59:49 p.m.					3,300 BCE
		Stone Age	Neolithic	Skill of writing, forging metal	
11:59:46 p.m.					5,000 BCE
			Mesolithic	Rise of agricultural techniques	
11:59:36 p.m.					10,000 BCE
11:59:06 p.m.	Pleistocene		Paleolithic	Neanderthal extinction 28 tya	
11:53:20 p.m.				Mitochondrial Eve 200–100 tya	
11:36:20 p.m.				Fire 700 tya	
Ca.11:00–11:30 p.m.				Homo Erectus 2 mya – 1 mya	
					2.5 mya

*BCE Before Christian Era
*tya thousand years ago
*mya million years ago

Brain

The average brain size of a *Homo sapiens* is today about 1350 cubic centimeters — three times that of our early bipedal ancestors.[8] When the first "archaic" mammals evolved two hundred thirty million years ago, their brains were four to five times that of a reptilian brain. Of modern mammals we may say that primates have brains about twice the size of other mammals. Apes have some of the largest primate brains, and human brains are about three times the size of the average

---

[8] Leakey, *The Origin of Humankind*, 43–48.

ape brain.[9] When seeking to distinguish human species from others, the size of our brain is at the top of the list.[10]

When we compare human brains with other brains we see what we share and what is unique to us. Besides the sheer size of the human brain relative to our overall size, the human brain has a larger forebrain, which is better for complex cognitive ability — that is, the cerebral cortex (necessary for language, problem solving, and other advanced thinking), is larger in the human being than in any other creature.

It is the brain itself that gives rise to another concept held dear by humans: that of the mind. The mind is where our internal thoughts reside. The mind is the center of consciousness. Nobody knows my mind unless I communicate it via speech, the written word, facial or other bodily expressions. Through my words here you may judge whether I am of *sound* mind. We know the human mind only through the medium of a single person. We are reminded that Aristotle thought the mind, rather than the soul, was eternal,[11] though precisely what he meant by *mind* is a matter of intense debate among philosophers.

The scientific study of the mind is called psychology, a relatively new field, founded in the late nineteenth and early twentieth centuries by Wundt (1832–1920), Freud (1856–1939), Jung (1875–1961), and others. The field has now expanded significantly to include brain research. New tools such as MRIs (magnetic resonance imaging devices) — unimaginable years ago — have contributed a great deal to our understanding. Through research and technology, we have been able to locate centers of various activities in the brain including vision, speech, memory (hippocampus), and even emotions such as fear, jealousy, and anger (amygdala). The field of psychology seems primed to grow exponentially in the twenty-first century with new knowledge to be gained by direct and measurable study of the human brain.

---

[9] Ibid., 142.

[10] While elephants and whales certainly have larger brains than that of humans, in relation to their size their brains are smaller. Some small mammals have brains that, relative to their size, are larger than the brains of human beings. The question of mammalian brain size relative to physical size has been the subject of much study. See Damir Janigro, ed., *Mammalian Brain Development*, Contemporary Neuroscience (New York: Humana Press, 2009); T. S. Kemp, *The Origin and Evolution of Mammals* (Oxford: Oxford University Press, 2003).

[11] Aristotle, *De An.* 3.5. 430a.

Emotion

Those who propose emotion as a unique human quality[12] probably don't have pets. Recent studies show that most, if not all, mammals have a somewhat developed amygdala, an almond shaped part of the limbic system in the brain, which is the center for emotion. In other words, mammals *can* sense fear and be angry. This is not news to pet owners, who often experience animals as remarkably intelligent creatures who possess and display emotion. Now brain research has confirmed the pet owners' hunch: emotion itself is not what makes us human. We will review an experiment and two stories from the news that demonstrate emotion in animals.

A recent experiment regarding inequity aversion sought to determine whether a dog might experience jealousy. If dogs are able to perceive inequity, are they averse to it? One dog, we will refer to him as Buck, received a reward for giving the paw, a relatively simple task for a domesticated dog. Later Buck continued to give the paw but was not given a reward. Even so, he continued to perform the trick several times. Still later, a second dog, Willy, was brought within sight of Buck. Now each of the two dogs was given a treat for giving the paw. After this pattern was established, another change was made. Even though both gave paw, only Willy received the treat. When this happened, Buck stopped giving paw almost immediately. In fact, he stopped participating much sooner than when he was the sole dog who did not receive positive reinforcement. The result of the experiment gives credence to the idea that dogs experience an emotion we call jealousy. Buck knew it was not fair that even though both gave paw only Willy received the treat. For a dog owner, the idea that their pet may experience jealousy is certainly not a revelation, but it is interesting that the experiment confirms what many suspected.[13]

A recent news story from Germany described the scene at Allwetter Zoo in Muenster. A mother gorilla by the name of Gana continued to carry the body of her three-month-old baby who died several days

---

[12] In the nineteenth century, some philosophers (e.g., Charles Bell, 1774–1842) proposed emotion as uniquely human. Darwin opposed him in his influential *The Expression of the Emotions in Man and Animals* (1872).

[13] The entire experiment, summarized here for our purposes, is published by F. Range, L. Horn, Z. Viranvi, and L. Huber, "The Absence of Reward Induces Inequity Aversion in Dogs," PNAS 106, no. 1 (2009): 340–45.

earlier. The zookeeper indicated that this behavior is not uncommon but part of the natural grieving process.[14]

Such stories of care and concern expressed by mammals for their young are not unique. Perhaps a more intriguing story comes from the Elephant Sanctuary in Hohenwald, Tennessee. The sanctuary receives endangered Asian and African elephants. These elephants often pair up and spend their time together, but one elephant, Tarra, bonded with Bella, a stray dog. They had been eating, drinking, sleeping, and playing together for years until Bella suffered a severe injury that left her without the ability to move her legs or wag her tail. She remained in special quarters for three weeks, during which time Tarra waited outside, concerned about her friend. When Bella was moved to the window to be seen by Tarra, Bella began wagging her tail. The staff moved Bella to be with Tarra, who touches or even "rubs" Bella's belly with her enormous elephant foot. The story was featured on CBS, which provided remarkable images of the two creatures.[15]

We might not be surprised to learn that all mammals have an amygdala, the part of the brain that processes fear, jealousy, and anger. Emotions are centered in the limbic system, a part of the brain common to mammals. Though human beings care for our young and for others, even this is not unique to our species. As we learn more and more about the living world around us, we may be surprised to see how similar, rather than different, we are to many creatures. Humanity is more a part of nature than apart from nature.

The Anthropic Principle

Many claim that our species is unique, special, or somehow the very purpose of creation. Anthropologists, cosmologists, and other scientists refer to this idea as the "anthropic principle." Though the term itself is fairly new (having been introduced in 1974) it can be

---

[14] "Mama Gorilla Won't Let Go of Her Dead Baby" *Associated Press* (August 2008) http://www.msnbc.msn.com/id/26316788.

[15] Steve Hartman, "On Elephant Sanctuary, Unlikely Friends," *CSB News* (November 2010), http://www.cbsnews.com/stories/2009/01/02/assignment_america/main4696340.shtml. Bella has since died (October 26, 2011).See The Elephant Sanctuary's website, www.elephants.com.

used in a wide variety of ways. There are primarily two variations of the anthropic principle referred to as the *weak* anthropic principle (that conditions observed in the universe allow the observer to exist) and the *strong* anthropic principle (the existence and emergence of intelligent life was somehow inevitable due to the structure of the universe). Some see a corollary of the strong anthropic principle that there must be a purpose or a meaning to human existence in the world. The world exists the way it does to support human life. Slight changes would make the earth itself sterile. Thus, humanity must be the goal or purpose of creation. Another corollary of the anthropic principle is that evolution produces higher order beings, and we as humans are the pinnacle of creation. The idea that human beings are the purpose of creation cannot be proved or disproved by science, but some perspective gained from our understanding of evolution might be instructive.

Dinosaurs reigned on the earth for over one hundred fifty million years. Supposing we could have asked the question and received a response, might the *Tyrannosaurus rex* have believed it was the purpose of creation? Human beings (depending on how we define the term) have been on this earth for about two million years, or defined in a more limited sense, perhaps two hundred thousand or even forty thousand years. Science may not tell us which creature is the purpose of creation, but it, specifically the fossil record, does tell us that other species have been on this earth much longer than we have. We know now that the world has been warmer and cooler throughout its history. The continents and oceans are moving on their tectonic plates and have been for millions of years. There have been five mass extinctions of the species and no reason there won't be another. Just as dinosaurs were extinguished about sixty-five million years ago, allowing mammals to dominate, so too may mammals become extinct, giving way to the reign of the insects or some other group. Indeed, entire television series have been produced based on this very concept.

Instead of thinking of humanity as the purpose of creation, perhaps it is better to recognize that our species is the only one to think at a highly abstract level. We are the only species to seek meaning — whether by religion, philosophy, science, or some other means. Our brains, and thus our minds, have developed incredible capabilities. Life has existed on this blue planet for more than 3.5 billion years. But only in the past five thousand years has one species, *Homo sapiens*, developed writing, civilization, philosophy, culture, and articulated a belief that there *is* life after death.

The Experience of Death

The following pastoral experience sets the stage for our next discussion.

The strident sound of his cell phone pierced the chaplain's peaceful sleep. Another call from the hospital. He was needed immediately and so he traveled the barren streets quickly to arrive at the neonatal unit. There he saw a young couple, the mother cradling a newborn infant. She was rocking back and forth whispering, "Don't die, Joshua. Don't die, Joshua. Don't die, Joshua." The father was hovering about, powerless, silent. Later that morning little Joshua died. The chaplain had no words of consolation, had no words of wisdom. Indeed, he had no words at all.

Though all living things die, making death an inevitable part of life, human beings often experience death as a problem. In the Old Testament, death was a problem for which God was not to blame. The book of Wisdom claims "Because God did not make death, nor does he rejoice in the destruction of the living. For he fashioned all things that they might have being" (1:13-14a; NABRE). In his letter to the Romans, Paul indicates that death came into the world through sin (Rom 5:12). No less an authority of Jesus himself is portrayed in the gospels as saying "[God] is not the God of the dead, but of the living" (Matt 22:32; Mark 12:27; Luke 20:38). Throughout the scriptures, death is most often portrayed negatively. The reason for death in the world is assigned to human beings and their sinfulness. Indeed, some Christian theologians claimed that had Adam not sinned there would not have been death. Both the Old and the New Testament express what may be a universal human hope: the death of death (Isa 25:8; 1 Cor 15:26, 55).

For a moment, let us prescind from the question of a human's death and focus instead on the biological notion of death. The term itself refers to the permanent cessation of an organism's vital functions. Death is a necessary and integral part of the cycle of life. We are reminded of the ecosystem's cycle of life and the food chain that we learned in grade school. Each autumn, trees lose their leaves. The leaves die, falling to the ground to protect and nourish seeds from the very same tree. When the tree itself dies, it decomposes and becomes nourishment for other living things. All plants and animals participate in this cycle. Indeed, everything we consume comes from living things: fruits, vegetables, meats, grains, etc. Death and the cycle of life have been a reality on this earth since living things existed. Seen from a biological point of view, death is not necessarily negative, though we certainly experience the death of a loved one, a fellow human being, or other living things as negative.

Human beings are not the only creatures to experience death as negative, or at least as a loss. As we have seen, many animals, especially mammals, perceive the death of another as a loss or a kind of privation. Does any other species besides ours contemplate its own death, the death of the self?[16] Does the mother gorilla cradling the dead baby know that she, too, will someday meet the same end? Though most animals have a self-preservation instinct, that instinct may not be the same as an awareness of its own death. As indicated in footnote 16, orangutans but not dogs seemed to possess self-awareness as determined by the mirror experiment. It is a great stretch from being merely self-aware to being aware of one's own mortality — until evidence suggests otherwise, it seems humans may be the only species on the planet to have this awareness.

Limiting ourselves strictly to scientific, verifiable, external, observable data, it seems that once a thing dies, it *is* no longer. Plants, dinosaurs, Neanderthals, dogs, and even human beings all face the same end: death. The corpse degenerates and the cycle of life continues. We have absolutely no scientific data to lead us to think otherwise.[17]

---

[16] Some might question whether mammals are even self-aware. Some psychologists have proposed "self-awareness" as a uniquely human trait. A "mirror experiment" with mammals would test the theory. When a dog looks at itself in the mirror does it know that it is seeing a reflection of itself? Or does it think that it is seeing another dog? The psychologists pasted a red circle to the dog's forehead, surmising that if the dog knew it was looking at a reflection, it would attempt to remove the red dot. The dog did not attempt to remove the red dot, but curiously, the orangutan did. This experiment and others like them remind us of how much we have in common with animals, especially mammals.

[17] The question about death is not merely a philosophical one. How we answer this question has a ramification for the treatment of the sick and dying, and for those in a vegetative state. We all know cases, such as Terry

No living thing, once dead, has returned to tell us what that death is like. We do not know what happens after death, as the Vatican Council Fathers noted: "It is when faced with death that the enigma of the human condition is most evident" (GS 18).

Although philosophers in the past century have claimed what the ancient world, including, of course, much of the ancient biblical world, took for granted—that there is no life after death[18]—a significant majority (74 percent) of those in the United States maintain some belief in an afterlife.[19] For many centuries, and for most of the period of the Old Testament, human beings have been able to live full and happy lives without postulating life after death. Why have we postulated it? And why do we cling to it so fiercely? The theological development of the afterlife has happened in a variety of faith traditions for a variety of reasons.[20]

Sixty thousand years ago, near the Zagros mountains of present-day Northern Iraq (Kurdistan), a Neanderthal was buried with a bundle of flowers at the entrance to a cave, known today as the

---

Schiavo and others, for whom this question is (or was) especially pertinent. As our science and medical technology progresses, we will continue to push the limits of life and death.

In 1980 the Uniform Determination of Death Act was introduced to standardize the way death is determined in the United States. This act was approved by the President's Commission on Medical Ethics, the American Medical Association, the American Bar Association, and the National Conference of Commissioners on Uniform State Laws. The act states that "an individual who has sustained either (1) irreversible cessation of circulatory and respiratory functions, or (2) irreversible cessation of all functions of the entire brain, including the brain stem is dead. A determination of death must be made in accordance with accepted medical standards." The law is accepted by all fifty states and the District of Columbia.

[18] E.g., Bertrand Russell, "Do We Survive Death?" in *Why I Am Not a Christian* (New York: Simon & Schuster, 1957), 88–93. See too the work of popular authors such Christopher Hitchens and Richard Dawkins.

[19] The Pew Forum on Religion and Public Life, "U.S. Religious Landscape Survey" (June 2008): 10, religions.pewforum.org/pdf/report2-religious-landscape-study-full.pdf.

[20] C.f. Alan Segal, *Life After Death: A History of the Afterlife in Western Religion* (New York: Doubleday, 2004) and Christopher M. Moreman, *Beyond the Threshold: Afterlife Beliefs and Experiences in World Religions* (Lanham, MA: Rowman & Littlefield, 2010).

Shanidar cave.[21] This particular Neanderthal burial is not unique. The oldest Neanderthal burial dates from one hundred thousand years ago. Why did Neanderthals bury their dead? Was burial a part of the grief process? With average brain sizes larger than modern humans, what did the Neanderthals mean to do by burying their dead? What meaning did they give to death? Would Neanderthals have made a claim to life after death had they been able?

How does our modern understanding of the human being, its evolution, the complicated relationship between brain, mind, and emotion, the very fact that we are here on this earth asking these questions, and the awareness of our own mortality, affect our theology and understanding of an afterlife?

A Possible Synthesis

What might we imagine if we contemplate the Christian message in twenty-first century terms? The age and scale of the universe might cause us to consider that humanity is not the sole purpose of creation. There is room for life in this great cosmos beyond what we find on the earth. In recognizing this, we are not so much reducing our understanding of humanity as enhancing our appreciation for the greatness and goodness of God.

The fundamental relationship between time and space might cause us to consider that any life after death is truly beyond space and time. To speak of life outside the bounds of our apparently stable three-dimensional world and a fourth dimension of time gives us pause. We know that there are aspects of this everyday world we cannot perceive, like ultraviolet or infrared light. Physicists tell us that the world may indeed be multidimensional, beyond what we can perceive. Is it so far-fetched to imagine that there are dimensions we cannot perceive? New life, a life after death, transcends the dimensions of space and time; it transcends the space-time continuum.

As a creature develops a mind, which can be understood as a function of brain size relative to overall size, the mind allows that creature to perceive things in new ways. Larger brains allow not only for emotion but also for forethought, self-awareness, and self-transcendence. But perhaps the larger brain size perceives something

---

[21] Leakey, *The Origin of Humankind*, 155.

more. Do we perceive a reality that we cannot quite express? As a species, perhaps we are emerging into a new horizon. We seem to be conscious of something beyond ourselves. A fish may see the effects of rain on the surface of the water and not understand the atmospheric cycle that produces that rain. The slug senses light but does not see images. The dog sees but only in black and white. Perhaps we sense something more than this world, though we cannot express it distinctly. So, too, do we have inklings of life after death, even if we do not clearly perceive what that involves or entails. "For now we see through a glass, darkly" (1 Cor 13:2; KJV).

Evolution shows us that single-celled organisms become multicellular and multicellular become responsive. Responsive beings become self-determinative. Self-determinative beings become free. Free beings become knowing, knowing becomes loving, and loving seeks the eternal. Could we be witnessing not only the evolution of biology but also the evolution of our own spirituality, our own self-transcendence? There is something in humanity that yearns to live forever, that craves the death of death. We want the loving relationships we have created, sustained, and nourished in this life to endure. We seem to be groping toward something for which we do not have adequate language. Poetry, music, song, and art reflect our best expressions of this desire.

We are the only species on this planet to declare that there is life after death. We have made this declaration only in the past two to three thousand years. As humans, we share a hope that we will live again. Most of us want to live a life where there is no pain, suffering, injustice, or hatred. The metaphorical term for that life is heaven. It is the prayer of the Lord: your kingdom come, your will be done, on earth as it is in heaven. The prayer essentially claims "God your kingdom in heaven is a place where there is no pain, no suffering, no injustice, no hatred. God, make it like that here on earth." We are invited into the process by which earth is made into heaven. The inbreaking of the kingdom happens now, when we choose to act justly, love tenderly, walk humbly (cf. Micah 6:8).

Conclusion

As a result of this brief study we have reviewed several factors critical to understanding resurrection in the modern world:

1. Neither "resurrection of the body" nor "resurrection of the flesh" occur in the bible, but "resurrection from the dead" does.
2. Resurrection of the body/flesh language was developed to cope with the philosophical and anthropological presuppositions of the second and third centuries and was repeated in subsequent centuries down to our modern era.
3. Paul, perhaps the only New Testament author to have witnessed the risen Christ, never describes the experience.
4. Paul's statements about his experience can legitimately be read to support an intangible, though no less real, experience of the risen Christ.
5. The earliest gospel, Mark, ends with an empty tomb and no appearance narrative.
6. Matthew and Luke, both of whom rely on Mark as a source, give more graphic details about the resurrected Christ.
7. The Gospel of John, which shows evidence of heavily redacted resurrection narratives, portrays the risen Christ tangibly.
8. Resurrection itself is a metaphor to speak of what happened to Jesus after his death.
9. There are many other metaphors used in the New Testament to speak of what happened to Jesus after his death.
10. Our modern world no longer uses the philosophical, anthropological, cosmological systems that were in place when some of the theological terminology was being forged.

So we are faced with a question: Are we able to speak to the contemporary world in an intelligent way about faith using modern terms while still being faithful to the apostolic witness?

By now it is clear that the risen Christ is more than revivified flesh. We may suppose that "resurrection of the flesh" language is inadequate to express to a modern Christian the mystery that the first Christians encountered in the risen Christ. Simply by using the term "flesh" we conjure up images of a graphically physical nature. Today, unlike in antiquity, we know that nearly every cell in the human body is regenerated at least every seven years. With over one hundred trillion cells in a human body, continually degenerating, generating, and regenerating, what precise flesh will be raised? As the German theologian Wilhelm Bruening claimed, "God loves more than the molecules that happen to be in the body at the time of death."[1] We cannot simply deny, as Methodius did, that food causes organic change. We understand that "we are what we eat." When we proclaim a resurrection of the flesh today the question often comes back to the famous chain consumption argument that Methodius addressed, or we delve into questions that vexed other theologians (regarding hair, blood, sweat, aborted fetuses, age, appearance, weight, even gender). Though the term "resurrection of the flesh" was certainly used in Christian history, was appropriate for earlier ages, and is a worthy subject of historical and theological study, it no longer conveys Christian theology accurately to a modern audience. The historical, philosophical, and anthropological groundwork that must be understood by a modern audience in order to understand properly the term resurrection of the flesh is a catechetical burden too high to hurdle effectively and often.

Resurrection of the body language seems likewise inadequate. The term does not even appear in the New Testament but is a later development as we saw. The modern Christian shares with the Corinthians the question "with what sort of body will they come?" We can be reminded of Paul's answer in 1 Corinthians 15:36, *aphrōn*, "fool." What we sow is a bare kernel. It must be transformed. Flesh and blood shall not inherit the kingdom of God. The early Christian testimony to the empty tomb is not simply an interesting detail "but is essential to understanding a major aspect in Christian theology, namely, that what God creates is not destroyed but is re-created and

---

[1] Bruening quoted in Hans Kung, *Eternal Life? Life after Death as a Medical, Philosophical, and Theological Problem,* trans. Edward Quinn (Garden City, NY: Doubleday, 1984), 111.

transformed."[2] As then-cardinal Joseph Ratzinger noted in his monumental *Introduction to Christianity*, "One thing at any rate may be fairly clear: both John (6:53) and Paul (1 Cor 15:50) state with all possible emphasis that the 'resurrection of the flesh,' the 'resurrection of the body' is not a 'resurrection of physical bodies.'"[3] So while it is certainly appropriate to study these terms in Christian theological history, if we continue to use them in catechetical or pastoral settings we may do more to undermine or unsettle faith than to build it up.

Ultimately, questions about the appearance of the resurrected body do not contribute to the profundity of the resurrection; rather, they drag it into the mire of the ridiculous, as Jerome himself experienced:

> And to those of us who ask whether the resurrection will exhibit from its former condition hair and teeth, the chest and the stomach, hands and feet, and other joints, then, no longer able to contain themselves and their jollity, they burst out laughing and adding insult to injury they ask if we shall need barbers, and cakes, and doctors, and cobblers, and whether we believe that the genitalia of which sex would rise, whether our [men's] cheeks would rise rough, while women's would be soft and whether the bodies would be differentiated based on sex. Because, if we surrender this point, they immediately proceed to female genitalia and everything else in and around the womb. They deny that singular members of the body rise, but the body, which is constituted from members, they say rises.[4]

We would do well to recognize that "resurrection of the flesh" and "resurrection of the body" language are post–New Testament, carrying the baggage of later second and third century philosophical and theological debates. That language echoed through the centuries so that the catechism of the Catholic Church quotes the Council of Lyons in claiming a resurrection of the flesh. Even so, the same catechism also states quite plainly that:

---

[2] Raymond Brown, *The Gospel According to John: XIII–XXI*, AB 29A (New York: Doubleday, 1970), 978.

[3] Joseph Ratzinger, *Introduction to Christianity*, trans. J. R. Foster (New York, NY: Herder and Herder, 1971), 277.

[4] *Epistula* 84.5 (CSEL 55, 127); translation mine.

> Christ's Resurrection was not a return to earthly life, as was
> the case with the raisings from the dead that he had performed
> before Easter: Jairus' daughter, the young man of Naim, Laza-
> rus. These actions were miraculous events, but the persons mi-
> raculously raised returned by Jesus' power to ordinary earthly
> life. At some particular moment they would die again. Christ's
> Resurrection is essentially different. In his risen body he passes
> from the state of death to another life beyond time and space. At
> Jesus' Resurrection his body is filled with the power of the Holy
> Spirit: he shares the divine life in his glorious state, so that St.
> Paul can say that Christ is "the man of heaven" (646).

Rather than speculate on the fantastical properties of resurrected
flesh, it seems better to recover and retain a focus on resurrection from
the dead. In so doing, theology would benefit from the insights of
biblical studies, scholars who study scripture, the "soul of theology"
(DV 24). For we must not allow "childish or arbitrary images to be
considered truths of faith."[5] Theologians, pastors, and others do not
need to give physical descriptions of the resurrected body, as Pope
John Paul II himself implored,

> In the context of Revelation, we know that the "heaven" or "hap-
> piness" in which we will find ourselves is neither an abstraction
> nor a physical place in the clouds, but a living, personal rela-
> tionship with the Holy Trinity. It is our meeting with the Father
> which takes place in the risen Christ through the communion
> of the Holy Spirit. It is always necessary to maintain a certain
> restraint in describing these "ultimate realities" since their de-
> piction is always unsatisfactory. Today, personalist language is
> better suited to describing the state of happiness and peace we
> will enjoy in our definitive communion with God.[6]

Today's pastors and preachers might echo the claim of Paul, "we
shall always be with the Lord" (1 Thess 4:17b; NABRE). As to what
that being with the Lord is like, we can hardly say. We know that we
will be with the Lord but we know not *how*. The future life is related
to this one as the oak is to the acorn (1 Cor 15:35-41); there is identity,

---

[5] *LOCQCE.*

[6] General Audience, (July 21, 1999), 4, http://www.vatican.va/holy_father
/john_paul_ii/audiences/1999/documents/hf_jp-ii_aud_21071999_en.html.

yet transformation and change. We can interpret resurrection from the dead, therefore, to be resurrection of the self rather than a resurrection of the flesh, or perhaps a resurrection to new life rather than a resurrection of the body. The self, the consciousness, the mind, the human person is raised to new life. By shifting the language in this way we respect the apostolic witness, the New Testament evidence, and we may also speak more convincingly to a modern age.

In addition to "resurrection to new life," what other language might be appropriate for today? What do we find in the New Testament to depict this new life with Christ? 1 Peter 1:13 speaks of a new birth. Paul tells us that all creation is groaning, awaiting the redemption that will be ours (Rom 8:22-23). 1 Timothy 4:8 speaks of a life for the future, our future true life (6:19). John speaks of life eternal (6:51, 58).

Indeed, resurrection itself is only one category by which to understand what happened to Jesus after his death. Exaltation, glory, seated at the right hand of God each convey essentially the same fundamental reality, but they are not necessarily physically graphic. Ultimately we are dealing with a metaphor. Failure to understand this will result in nonsensical notions of life after death that will be easily dismissed by today's educated audience. All of the New Testament images and metaphors point to a fundamental reality. We (together, not individually) shall be with God. We are not able to say precisely what that life entails. We are on the verge of a promise we cannot completely comprehend. "Eye has not seen nor ear heard . . . what God has prepared for those who love him" (1 Cor 2:9; translation mine).

Theological Epilogue

As Christians, Jesus Christ and the life he now lives with God is our guarantee for hope in life after death. Paul recognized that Christian faith gives one hope of an afterlife (1 Thess 4:13). Our Christian hope tells us that because God exalted Christ, God will exalt us too. Because God raised Christ from the dead, God will raise us from the dead too. Because Christ ascended into heaven, we too will ascend into heaven. Those who have died in Christ will live forever, for Christ is the first fruits of those who have fallen asleep. Just as we have borne the image of the man of earth, we shall bear the image of the heavenly man.

But rather than claim Christians will be the only ones to enjoy life eternal, our claim is that Christ is the guarantee of that hope for humanity. Indeed, there is no observable or verifiable data to indicate an afterlife. Instead, the data point to death as the end of a living thing—nothing else, only sleep without dreams. But because of the apostolic witness to Christ's new life, we have the courage to proclaim a hope not accessible to observation or scientific verification. Life will be changed, not ended (1 Cor 15:51). In personalist language, it is my Christian hope that the same grace that created me and brought me into being will, by another free gift of grace, raise me and others up to a new life with Christ.

Appendix A

Table 1 Attestations to the Risen Christ

Category		Scripture citations	
1	Jesus being raised	1 Cor 15:3-7; Rom 1:3-4; 4:25; Mark 8:31; Acts 2:23-24; 4:10; 5:30-31; 10:39-40	Straightforward, kerygmatic statements
2	Jesus appearing	1 Cor 15:5-8; Luke 24:34	Straightforward, kerygmatic statements
3	Finding the tomb empty	Matt 28:1-8; Mark 16:1-8; Luke 24:1-12, 24; John 20:1-13	Narrative stating the body is not in the tomb
4	Personal eye-witness testimony from a New Testament author	Gal 1:16; 1 Cor 9:1; 15:8	Statement, little to no elaboration
5	Appearance narratives		Narratives, no chronological order
	A. Mary Magdalene/ Women	Matt 28:9-10; Mark 16:9-11; John 20:14-18	
	B. Two Disciples	Mark 16:12-13; Luke 24:13-35	
	C.1. Assembled Disciples (Jerusalem)	Mark 16:14; Luke 24:36-43; John 20:19-20, 26-29	
	C.2.a Eleven Disciples (Galilee)	Matt 28:16-18	
	C.2.b Seven Disciples (Sea of Tiberias)	John 21:1-23	
	D. Commissioning of Disciples	Matt 28:19-20; Mark 16:15-18; Luke 24:44-49; John 20:21-23; Acts 1:6-8	
	E. Ascension	Mark 16:19-20; Luke 24:50-53; Acts 1:9-12	

Table 2

Threefold description of Paul's call in Acts; emphasis mine.

NRSV Acts 9:1-20	NRSV Acts 22:1-16	NRSV Acts 26:1-20
Meanwhile Saul, still breathing threats and murder against the disciples of the Lord,	"Brothers and fathers, listen to the defense that I now make before you." When they heard him addressing them in Hebrew, they became even more quiet. Then he said: "I am a Jew, born in Tarsus in Cilicia, but brought up in this city at the feet of Gamaliel, educated strictly according to our ancestral law, being zealous for God, just as all of you are today. I persecuted this Way up to the point of death by binding both men and women and putting them in prison,	Agrippa said to Paul, "You have permission to speak for yourself." Then Paul stretched out his hand and began to defend himself: "I consider myself fortunate that it is before you, King Agrippa, I am to make my defense today against all the accusations of the Jews, because you are especially familiar with all the customs and controversies of the Jews; therefore I beg of you to listen to me patiently. "All the Jews know my way of life from my youth, a life spent from the beginning among my own people and in Jerusalem. They have known for a long time, if they are willing to testify, that I have belonged to the strictest sect of our religion and lived as a Pharisee. And now I stand here on trial on account of my hope in the promise made by God to our ancestors, a promise that our twelve tribes hope to attain, as they

		earnestly worship day and night. It is for this hope, your Excellency, that I am accused by Jews! Why is it thought incredible by any of you that God raises the dead? "Indeed, I myself was convinced that I ought to do many things against the name of Jesus of Nazareth.
went to the *high priest* and asked him for **letters** to the synagogues at **Damascus**, so that if he found any who belonged to the Way, men or women, he might bring them bound to **Jerusalem**.	as the *high priest* and the whole council of elders can testify about me. From them I also received **letters** to the brothers in **Damascus**, and I went there in order to bind those who were there and to bring them back to **Jerusalem** for *punishment*.	And that is what I did in Jerusalem; with authority received from the *chief priests*, I not only locked up many of the saints in prison, but I also cast my vote against them when they were being condemned to death. By *punishing* them often in all the synagogues I tried to force them to blaspheme; and since I was so furiously enraged at them, I pursued them even to foreign cities.
Now as he was going along and approaching **Damascus**, *suddenly* **a** **light from heaven** flashed **around him**.	"While I was on my way and approaching **Damascus**, **about noon** a great **light from heaven** *suddenly* shone **about me**.	"With this in mind, I was traveling to **Damascus** with the authority and commission of the chief priests, **when** **at midday** along the road, your Excellency, I saw **a light from heaven**, brighter than the sun, shining **around me** and my companions.

NRSV Acts 9:1-20	NRSV Acts 22:1-16	NRSV Acts 26:1-20
He **fell** **to the ground and heard a voice saying to him,** "**Saul, Saul, why do you persecute me?**"	I **fell** **to the ground and heard a voice saying to me,** 'Saul, Saul, why are you persecuting me?'	When we had all **fallen to the ground, I heard a voice saying to me** in the Hebrew language, '**Saul, Saul, why are you persecuting me?** It hurts you to kick against the goads.'
He asked, "**Who are you, Lord?**" The reply came, "**I am Jesus, whom you are persecuting.**	I answered, '**Who are you, Lord?**' Then he said to me, '**I am Jesus** of Nazareth **whom you are persecuting.**'	I asked, '**Who are you, Lord?**' The Lord answered, '**I am Jesus whom you are persecuting.**
But **get up** and *enter the city*, and **you will be told** what **you** are **to do.**"	I asked, 'What am I to do, Lord?' The Lord said to me, '**Get up** and *go to Damascus*; there **you will be told** everything that has been assigned to **you to do**.'	But **get up** and stand on your feet; for I have appeared to you for this purpose, to appoint you to serve and testify to the things in which you have seen me and to those in which I will appear to you. I will rescue you from your people and from the Gentiles—to whom I am sending you to open their eyes so that they may turn from darkness to light and from the power of Satan to God, so that they may receive forgiveness of sins and

		a place among those who are sanctified by faith in me.'
The men **who were** traveling **with him** stood speechless because they heard the voice but saw no one. Saul got up from the ground, and though his eyes were open, **he could** *see nothing*; so *they* led him by the **hand** and *brought him* into **Damascus**.	Now *those* **who were with me** saw the light but did not hear the voice of the one who was speaking to me. Since **I could** *not see* because of the brightness of that light, *those who were with me* took my **hand** and *led me* to **Damascus**.	
For three days he was without sight, and neither ate nor drank.		
Now there was **a** disciple in Damascus named **Ananias**. The Lord said to him in a vision, "Ananias." He answered, "Here I am, Lord." The Lord said to him, "Get up and go to the street called Straight, and at the house of Judas look for a man of Tarsus named Saul. At this moment he is praying, and he has seen in a vision a man named Ananias come in and lay his hands on him so that he might	"**A** certain **Ananias**, who was a devout man according to the law and well spoken of by all the Jews living there,	

NRSV Acts 9:1-20	NRSV Acts 22:1-16	NRSV Acts 26:1-20
regain his sight." But Ananias answered, "Lord, I have heard from many about this man, how much evil he has done to your saints in Jerusalem; and here he has authority from the chief priests to bind all who invoke your name." But the Lord said to him, "Go, for he is an instrument whom I have chosen to bring my name before Gentiles and kings and before the people of Israel; I myself will show him how much he must suffer for the sake of my name."		
So Ananias **went** and entered the house. **He** laid his hands on Saul and **said,** "**Brother Saul**, the Lord Jesus, who appeared to you on your way here, has sent me so that you may **regain your sight** and be filled with the Holy Spirit." And immediately something like scales fell from his eyes, and his **sight** was *restored*.	**came** to me; and standing beside me, **he** **said,** '**Brother Saul**, **regain your sight!**' In that very hour I *regained* my **sight** and saw him.	
	Then he said, 'The God of our ancestors has chosen you to	

	know his will, to see the Righteous One and to hear his own voice; for you will be his witness to all the world of what you have seen and heard.	
Then he **got up** and **was baptized,**	And now why do you delay? **Get up, be baptized,** and have your sins washed away, calling on his name.'	
and after taking some food, he regained his strength. For several days he was with the disciples in **Damascus,** and immediately he began to proclaim Jesus in the synagogues, saying, "He is the Son of God."		"After that, King Agrippa, I was not disobedient to the heavenly vision, but declared first to those in **Damascus,** then in Jerusalem and throughout the countryside of Judea, and also to the Gentiles, that they should repent and turn to God and do deeds consistent with repentance.

Table 3   Finding the Tomb Empty (Synoptics)
Emphasis mine.

NABRE Mark 16:1-8	NABRE Matthew 28:1-8	NABRE Luke 24:1-12
When **the sabbath** was over, Mary Magdalene, Mary, the mother of James, and Salome bought spices so that they might go and anoint him. Very early when the sun had risen, on the **first day of the week**, they **came to the tomb**. They were saying to one another, "Who will roll back the stone for us from the entrance to the tomb?"	After **the sabbath**, as the **first day of the week** was dawning, Mary Magdalene and the other Mary **came to see the tomb**.	But at daybreak on the **first day of the week** they took the spices they had prepared and **went to the tomb**.
When they looked up, they saw that the **stone had been rolled back**; *it was very large.*	And behold, *there was a great earthquake; for an angel of the Lord descended from heaven,* approached, **rolled back the stone**, and sat upon it.	They found **the stone rolled away** from the tomb;
On entering the tomb they saw a *young man sitting on the right side, clothed in a white robe,* and they were utterly amazed.	*His appearance was like lightning and his clothing was white as snow.* The guards were shaken with fear of him and became like dead men.	but **when they entered**, they did not find the body of the Lord Jesus. While they were puzzling over this, behold, *two men in dazzling garments appeared to them.* They were terrified and bowed their faces to the ground.
He said to them, "Do not be amazed! You seek Jesus of Nazareth, the	Then the angel said to the women in reply, "Do not be afraid! I know that you are	They said to them, "Why do you seek the living one among the dead? **He is not**

crucified. **He has been raised; he is not here**.	seeking Jesus the crucified. **He is not here**, for **he has been raised** just as he said.	**here**, but **he has been raised**. Remember what he said to you while he was still in Galilee, that the Son of Man must be handed over to sinners and be crucified, and rise on the third day." And they remembered his words.
Behold the place where they laid him. But go and tell his disciples and Peter, **'He is going before you to Galilee; there you will see him**, as he told you.'"	Come and see the place where he lay. Then go quickly and tell his disciples, '*He has been raised from the dead*, and **he is going before you to Galilee; there you will see him**.' Behold, I have told you."	
Then they went out and fled from the tomb, **seized with trembling and bewilderment**. They said nothing to anyone, **for they were afraid**.	Then they went away quickly from the tomb, **fearful** *yet overjoyed*, and ran to announce this to his disciples.	Then they returned from the tomb and announced all these things to the eleven and to all the others.
(cf 16:1) *Mary Magdalene, Mary, the mother of James, and Salome*	(cf 28:1) *Mary Magdalene and the other Mary*	The women were Mary Magdalene, Joanna, and Mary the mother of James; the others who accompanied them also told this to the apostles, but their story seemed like nonsense and they did not believe them.
		But Peter got up and ran to the tomb, bent down, and saw the burial cloths alone; then he went home amazed at what had happened.

Appendix B

Biblical Worldview

Heavenly Seat of the Divinity

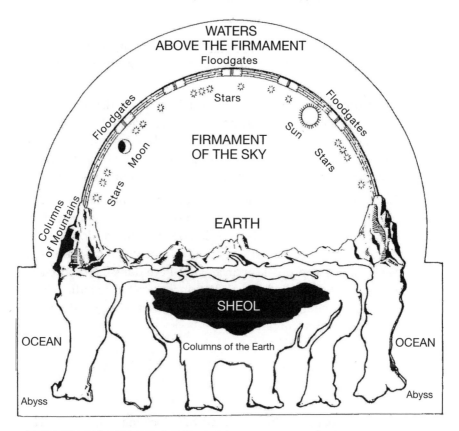

THE WORLD OF THE HEBREWS

THE WORLD OF THE HEBREWS—Graphic representation of the Hebrew conception of the world. God's heavenly seat rests above the superior waters. Below these waters lies the firmament or sky which resembles an overturned bowl and is supported by columns. Through the openings (floodgates) in its vault the superior waters fall down upon the earth in the form of rain or snow. The earth is a platfom resting on columns and surrounded by waters, the seas. Underneath the columns lie the inferior waters. In the depths of the earth is Sheol, the home of the dead (also called the nether world). This was the same prescientific concept of the universe as that held by the Hebrews' pagan neighbors.

Appendix C

S. Congrégation Pour la Doctrine de la Foi
La «Résurrection de la Chair»
Dans le Symbole des Apôtres

1. L'expression «carnis resurrectionem» du Symbole des apôtres a été traduite jusqu'à présent dans les diverses langues de façons différentes:
   - En traduisant à la lettre le texte latin du Symbole des apôtres (1);
   - En traduisant le mot «carnis» par un mot équivalent (2);
   - En traduisant le mot «mortuorum» pris dans le paragraphe «Et exspecto resurrectionem mortuorum» (et j'attends la résurrection des morts) du Symbole de Nicée-Constantinople (3).

2. La question de la traduction de l'expression «carnis resurrectionem» du Symbole des apôtres a été examinée par la S. Congrégation pour la Doctrine de la Foi qui, dans sa réunion ordinaire, a adopté les décisions qui suivent, accompagnées des raisons théologiques afférentes.

Ces décisions, approuvées par le Saint-Père dans l'audience accordée à S. Ém. le Cardinal Joseph Ratzinger, Préfet de ladite Congrégation, le 2 décembre 1983, ont été transmises à ce Dicastère par lettre du 14 décembre suivant.

Congrégation pour la Doctrine de la Foi

A. Décisions

1. Il n'existe pas *dans l'absolu* de raisons doctrinales contre la traduction «résurrection des morts», comme si cette formule n'exprimait pas la même foi que celle qui est exprimée par la formule «résurrection de la chair», mais il existe une convergence de raisons théologiques conjoncturelles qui militent pour le maintien de la traduction traditionnelle exacte (littérale).

2. Dans les futures traductions, à présenter à l'approbation ecclésiastique, on devra maintenir la traduction exacte traditionnelle.

3. Là où le changement a déjà été autorisé, il conviendra de communiquer aux évêques les raisons qui font *recommander* le retour à la traduction *exacte* traditionnelle.

B. Raisons théologiques et conjoncturelles

1. Les deux formules «résurrection des morts» et «résurrection de la chair» sont des expressions diverses et complémentaires de la même tradition primitive de l'Église, et par conséquent une prévalence exclusive ou totale de la formule «résurrection des morts» constituerait un appauvrissement doctrinal. Il est vrai en fait que cette dernière expression contient aussi implicitement l'affirmation de la résurrection corporelle, mais la formule «résurrection de la chair», comme *expression*, est plus explicite dans l'affirmation de cet aspect particulier de la résurrection, comme le démontre son origine même.

2. L'abandon de la formule «résurrection de la chair» comporte le danger de soutenir les théories actuelles qui placent la résurrection au moment de la mort, excluant en pratique la résurrection corporelle, spécialement de *cette* chair. Sur la diffusion, aujourd'hui, d'une telle vision «spiritualisante» de la résurrection, la S. Congrégation pour la Doctrine de la Foi a attiré l'attention des évêques dans sa lettre «sur quelques questions concernant l'eschatologie» du 17 mai 1979.

(1) Cf. les traductions en italien, français et portugais:
- «La risurrezione della carne» (*Missel romain*, Conf. épisc. italienne, 2e éd., 1983, p. 306);
- «La résurrection de la chair» (*Missel romain pour les pays francophones*, Paris 1974, p. 11);
- «A ressurreiçao da carne» (*Missel romain*, Conf. épisc. du Brésil, Rio de Janeiro 1973, p. 351).

(2) Cf. la traduction en anglais:
- «The resurrection of the body» (la résurrection du corps) (*Rituel romain: rite du baptême des enfants*, traduction anglaise approuvée par la Conf. épisc. des USA et confirmée par le Siège apostolique, New York 1970, p. 89).

(3) Cf. traduction en allemand et en espagnol (la résurrection des morts):
- «Die Auferstehung der Toten» (*Missel pour les diocèses de langue allemande*, 1974, lre partie, p. 119);
- «La resurreccion de los muertos» (*Livre du Secrétariat national de liturgie*, Madrid 1983, p. 394).

The Sacred Congregation for the Doctrine of the Faith[1]
The "Resurrection of the Flesh"
in the Apostles' Creed

1. The expression "carnis resurrectionem" in the Apostles' Creed has been translated into various languages in a variety of ways:

– In translating literally the Latin text of the Apostles' Creed (1);
– In translating the word "carnis" by an equivalent word (2);
– In translating the word "mortuorum" in the paragraph "Et exspecto resurrectionem mortuorum" (and I look for the resurrection of the dead) of the Niceo-Constantinopolitan Creed (3)

2. The question of the translation of the expression "carnis resurrectionem" of the Apostles' Creed has been examined by the Sacred Congregation for the Doctrine of the Faith which, in its regular meeting, has adopted the decisions which follow, accompanied by theological rationale statements.

These decisions, approved by the Holy Father in an audience granted to His Eminence Cardinal Joseph Ratzinger, Prefect of that Congregation, on December 2, 1983, were forwarded to this dicastery by letter on December 14.

Congregation for the Doctrine of the Faith

A. Decisions

1. There does not exist in the absolute any doctrinal reasons against translating "resurrection of the dead" as if this formula does not express the same faith which is expressed by the formula "resurrection of the flesh" but there does exist a convergence of conjectural theological reasons which militate for keeping the traditional exact (literal) translation.

2. In the future, translations that have been presented for ecclesiastical approval, will maintain the traditional exact translation.

3. Where change has already been authorized, the reasons why *recommending* a return to the traditional *exact* translation should be communicated to the bishops.

[1] Translation mine.

B. Theological and Conjectural Reasons

1. The two formulae "resurrection of the dead" and "resurrection of the flesh" are two diverse and complementary expressions for the same primitive tradition of the Church, and therefore an exclusive or total prevalence of the formula "resurrection of the dead" would constitute a doctrinal impoverishment. It is true indeed that the latter expression also implicitly contains the affirmation of the bodily resurrection, but the formula "resurrection of the flesh" as an *expression*, is more explicitly in the affirmation of this particular aspect of the resurrection, as demonstrated by its origin.

2. The abandonment of the formula "resurrection of the flesh" has the danger of supporting current theories that place the resurrection at the moment of death, excluding in practice the bodily resurrection, especially of *this* flesh. On the diffusion today of such a vision "spiritualizing" the resurrection, the Sacred Congregation for the Doctrine of the Faith has attracted the attention of the bishops in its letter "On Certain Questions Concerning Eschatology" of May 17, 1979.

(1) Cf. the translations in Italian, French, and Portugese:

- "The resurrection of the flesh" (*Roman Missal*, Italian Bishops Conference, 2 ed., 1983, p. 306);
- "The resurrection of the flesh" (*Roman Missal for the French-Speaking Countries*, Paris 1974, p. 11);
- "The resurrection of the flesh" (*Roman Missal*, Episcopal Conference of Brazil, Rio de Janeiro 1973, p. 351).

(2) Cf. The translation in English:

- "The resurrection of the body" (*Roman Ritual: Rite of Baptism for Infants*, English translation approved by Episcopal Conference of the USA and confirmed by the Apostolic See, New York 1970, p. 89).

(3) Cf. Translation in German and Spanish (the resurrection of the dead):

- "The Resurrection of the Dead" (*Missal for the Dioceses of the German Language*, 1974, 1st ed., p. 119);
- "The Resurrection of the Dead" (*Book of the National Secretariat of Liturgy*, Madrid 1983, p. 394).

Appendix D

	Resurrection/ Raised/Rise from the Dead	Sitting/ Seated/ Standing at God's Right Hand	Exalted/ Exaltation/ Being Lifted Up	Glorified/ Taken Up in Glory/ Enter into His Glory	Ascension (Taken Up/Lifted Up [into Heaven])	Going to the Father	Vindicated in the Spirit	In Paradise	Entering the Heavenly Holy of Holies
Matthew	16:21; 17:9, 23; 20:19; 27:53; 28:6, 7	22:44; 26:64							
Mark	8:31; 9:9, 31; 10:34; 14:28; 16:6, 9, 14	14:62; 16:19			16:19				
Luke	9:22; 18:33; 24:7, 34, 46	22:69		24:26	24:51			23:43	
John	2:22; 20:9; 21:14		3:14; 8:28; 12:32-34	7:39; 12:16, 23; 16:14; 17:4-5	20:17	14:12, 28; 16:5, 10, 17, 28			
Acts	1:22; 2:31, 32; 3:15, 26; 4:2, 10, 33; 5:30; 10:4, 40; 13:30, 33, 34, 37; 17:3, 31; 26:23	2:33, 34; 5:31; 7:55	2:33; 5:31	3:13	1:2, 9, 11, 22				
Romans	1:4; 4:24, 25; 6:5; 7:4; 8:11, 34; 10:9	8:34		8:17					
1 Corinthians	6:14; 15:12, 13, 15, 21								
2 Corinthians	4:14								

Book									
Galatians	1:1								
Ephesians	1:20; 2:6	1:20-21							
Philippians	3:10		2:9	3:21					
Colossians	2:12	3:1							
1 Thessalonians	1:10; 4:14								
2 Thessalonians									
1 Timothy				3:16	3:16		3:16		
2 Timothy	2:8								
Titus									
Philemon									
Hebrews	6:2	1:3, 13; 8:1; 10:12; 12:2		2:7, 9					9:12, 24-26
James									
1 Peter	1:3, 21; 3:21	3:22		1:21					
2 Peter				1:17					
1 John									
2 John									
3 John									
Jude									
Revelation									

Bibliography

Attridge, Harold. *Hebrews: A Commentary on the Epistle to the Hebrews.* Hermeneia. Minneapolis, MN: Fortress, 1989.

Brown, Raymond E. *The Gospel According to John: XIII–XXI.* AB 29A. New York: Doubleday, 1970.

Bultmann, Rudolf. *History of the Synoptic Tradition.* Revised ed. New York: Harper & Row, 1963.

———. *Theology of the New Testament.* 2 vols. London: SCM, 1952–55.

Bynum, Carolyn Walker. *The Resurrection of the Body in Western Christianity, 200–1336.* Cambridge: Cambridge University Press, 1995.

Callan, C. *The Epistles of Paul: 1. Romans, First and Second Corinthians, Galatians.* New York: Wagner, 1922.

Carlston, C. E. "Transfiguration and Resurrection." *JBL* 80 (1961): 233–40.

Catechismus ex Decreto Concilii Tridentini ad Parochos. Rome: Societas S. Joannis Evangelistae; Tournai: Desclée, 1902.

Cherniss, H. F. *The Platonism of Gregory of Nyssa.* UCPCP 11. Berkeley: University of California, 1930. Repr. New York: Burt Franklin, 1971.

Collins, Adela Yarbro. *Mark.* Hermeneia. Minneapolis, MN: Fortress, 2007.

Collins, John J. *Daniel.* Hermeneia. Minneapolis, MN: Fortress, 1993.

Daniélou, J. "La resurrection des corps chez Grégoire de Nysse." *VC* 7 (1953): 154–70.

Davies, J. G. "Factors Leading to the Emergence of Belief in the Resurrection of the Flesh." *JTS* 23 (1972): 448–55.

Dechow, J. F. *Dogma and Mysticism and in Early Christianity: Epiphanius of Cyprus and the Legacy of Origen.* PMS 13. Macon, GA: Mercer University, 1988.

Deferrari, R. J. *Hugh of Saint Victor on the Sacraments of the Christian Faith (De Sacramentis).* Cambridge, MA: The Mediaeval Academy of America, 1951.

Dennis, T. J. "Gregory on the Resurrection of the Body." In *The Easter Sermons of Gregory of Nyssa: Translation and Commentary,* 55–80. Edited by A. Spira and C. Klock. Cambridge, MA: Philadelphia Patristic Foundation, Ltd., 1981.

Dodd, C. H. "The Appearance of the Risen Christ: An Essay in Form Criticism of the Gospels." In *Studies in the Gospels,* 9–35. Edited by D. E. Nineham. Oxford: Oxford University Press, 1955.

Donfried, K. P. *The Setting of Second Clement in Early Christianity*. Leiden: E. J. Brill, 1974.

Elliott, J. H. *1 Peter*. AB 37B. New York: Doubleday, 2000.

Fitzmyer, Joseph A. *Acts of the Apostles*. AB 18C. New York: Doubleday, 1998.

———. "The Aramaic Background of Philippians 2:6-11." *CBQ* 3 (1988): 470–84.

———. *The Gospel According to Luke: X–XXIV*. AB 28A. New York: Doubleday, 1985.

Goudge, H. *The First Epistle to the Corinthians*. 5th rev. ed. London: Methuen, 1926.

Hall, Stephen S. "Last of the Neanderthals: Why Did Our Ice Age Rivals Vanish?" *National Geographic* 214, no. 4 (October 2008): 58.

Hay, D. M. *Glory at the Right Hand: Psalm 110 in Early Christianity*. SBLMS 18. Nashville: Abingdon, 1973.

Damir Janigro, ed. *Mammalian Brain Development*. Contemporary Neuroscience. New York: Humana Press, 2009.

Johnson, Luke Timothy. *The First and Second Letters to Timothy*. AB 35A. New York: Doubleday, 2001.

Kelhoffer, James A. *Miracle and Mission: The Authentication of Missionaries and Their Message in the Longer Ending of Mark*. Tübingen: Mohr-Siebeck, 2000.

Kelly, J. N. D. *Jerome: His Life, Writings, and Controversies*. Peabody, MA: Hendrickson, 1998.

Kemp, T. S. *The Origin and Evolution of Mammals*. Oxford: Oxford University Press, 2003.

Knopf, R. *Die Lehre der zwölf Apostel. Die zwei Clemensbriefe*. HNTE. Die Apostolischen Väter 1. Tübingen: Mohr-Siebeck, 1920.

Kung, Hans. *Eternal Life? Life after Death as a Medical, Philosophical, and Theological Problem*. Translated by Edward Quinn. Garden City, NY: Doubleday, 1984.

Leakey, Richard. *The Origin of Humankind*. New York: Basic Books (Harper Collins), 1994.

Leakey, Richard and Roger Lewin. *Origins Reconsidered: In Search of What Makes Us Human*. New York: Doubleday, 1992.

Lunine, Jonathan. *Earth: Evolution of a Habitable World*. Cambridge Atmospheric and Space Science Series. Cambridge: Cambridge University Press, 1998.

Luther, Martin. *Commentary on 1 Corinthians*. Edited by A. Leitzmann and O. Clemen. *Luthers Werke in Auswahl*. Vol 7. Berlin: W. de Gruyter, 1962.

MacRory, J. *The Epistles of St. Paul to the Corinthians*. 2 vols. St. Louis: B. Herder, 1915.

McWilliam-Dewart, J. E. *Death and Resurrection*. MFC 22. Wilmington, DE: M. Glazier, 1986.

Moreman, Christopher M. *Beyond the Threshold: Afterlife Beliefs and Experiences in World Religions*. Rowman & Littlefield, 2010.

Niederwimmer, K. *The Didache*. Hermeneia. Minneapolis, MN: Fortress, 1998.

Nolan, K. *The Immortality of the Soul and the Resurrection of the Body According to Giles of Rome: A Historical Study of a Thirteenth Century Theological Problem.* SEAug 1. Rome: Studium Theologicum Augustinianum, 1967.

Pew Forum on Religion and Public Life. "U.S. Religious Landscape Survey." (June 2008), p.10, religions.pewforum.org/pdf/report2-religious-landscape -study-full.pdf.

Pope, M. *Job.* AB 15. Garden City, NY: Doubleday, 1965.

Quasten, J. *Patrology.* 3 vols. Westminster, MD: Newman, 1950–60.

Rahner, K. "The Resurrection of the Body." In *Theological Investigations 2: Man in the Church.* Baltimore: Helicon, 1963.

Range, F., L. Horn, Z. Viranvi, and L. Huber. "The Absence of Reward Induces Inequity Aversion in Dogs." PNAS 106, no. 1 (2009): 340–45.

Ratzinger, J. *Introduction to Christianity.* Translated by J. R. Foster. New York: Herder and Herder, 1971.

Robinson, James M. "Jesus: From Easter to Valentinus (or the Apostles' Creed)." *JBL* 101 (1982): 5–37.

Russell, Bertrand. "Do We Survive Death?" In *Why I Am Not a Christian,* 88–93. New York: Simon & Schuster, 1957.

Sanders, E.P. *Paul.* Oxford: Oxford University Press, 1991.

Schep, J. A. *The Nature of the Resurrection Body.* Grand Rapids, MI: Eerdmans, 1964.

Schmisek, Brian. "Augustine's Use of 'Spiritual Body.'" *AugSt* 35, no. 2 (2004): 237–52.

———. "Paul's Vision of the Risen Lord." *BTB* 41, no. 2 (2011): 76–83.

———. "The Body of His Glory: Resurrection Imagery in Philippians 3:20-21." *BTB* 43, no. 1 (2013): 23–28.

Schoedel, W. R. *Ignatius of Antioch: A Commentary on the Letters of Ignatius of Antioch.* Hermeneia. Philadelphia: Fortress, 1985.

Segal, Alan. *Life after Death: A History of the Afterlife in Western Religion.* New York: Doubleday, 2004.

Stringer, Chris and Peter Andrews. *The Complete World of Human Evolution.* New York: Thames & Hudson, 2005.

Trigg, J. W. *Origen.* The Early Church Fathers. New York: Routledge, 1998.

Weisheipl, J. A. *Friar Thomas D'Aquino: His Life, Thought, and Works.* Washington, DC: Catholic University of America, 1983.

Scripture Index

Subject Index